EVERYTHING
BUT
MONEY

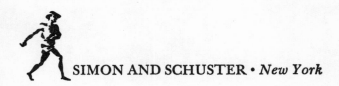 *by Sam Levenson*

SIMON AND SCHUSTER • *New York*

To brother Bill

✿✿✿✿ ACKNOWLEDGMENTS

THIS BOOK HAS BEEN A FAMILY PROJECT. I am profoundly indebted to my wife for discussing ideas with me; to my daughter Emily for reading the manuscript aloud to me and to anyone else who would listen; to my son Conrad for his points of view; to brother Albert and his good wife Helen for typing; to Uncle Harry and Aunt Beth also for typing; to Emily's friend Philip for more typing; to Emily's friend Susie for her frank teenage reactions.

I owe special thanks to Peter Matson for bringing the book to the attention of Simon and Schuster; to Charlotte Seitlin of Simon and Schuster for patient direction and editing; to Charlotte Greene for much good advice; to an old friend, Dave Vern, who as far back as twenty years ago sat around and exchanged reminiscences with me about our folk heritage; to a very special friend, Sarah Stieglitz, for reading and advising.

To my brothers and sister, and to all the sisters-in-law, for the memories which found their way into the book.

Thanks to the editors of all of the following for the right to use, in revised form, pieces or parts of pieces which I wrote for the New York *Herald Tribune*, *TV Guide*, *Variety*, *Congress Weekly*, *Commentary*, the New York *Mirror Magazine*, *Parents' Magazine*, *This Week*, *Coronet* Magazine, *Collier's*, the *Metropolitan Star*, Chicago *American* and *United Press International*; also to Herb Kamm, managing editor of the New York *World-Telegram & Sun*, and to Nat Fields.

I
Sweet Horseradish

My PARENTS CAME TO AMERICA by invitation. Those who had landed here before them sent back picture post-cards of a lady called Miss Liberty. Printed on them were these words:

> Give me your tired, your poor,
> Your huddled masses yearning to breathe free,
> The wretched refuse of your teeming shore.
> Send these, the homeless, tempest-tost to me,
> I lift my lamp beside the golden door!

It was signed Emma Lazarus, a name that sounded familiar to my parents—perhaps some second cousin on my mother's side. So Mama and Papa packed all their belongings and left for America. After all, who was more tired, poor, huddled, yearning to be free, wretched, homeless and tempest-tost than they?

I was raised as a virtually free American in East Harlem, a section of New York that was called a slum by sightseeing guides and a depressed area by sociologists. Both were right. Our neighborhood fulfilled all the sordid requirements with honors. We were unquestionably above average in squalid tenements, putrid poolrooms, stenchy saloons, cold flats, hot roofs, dirty streets and flying garbage. Yet, paradoxically, I never felt depressed or deprived. My environment was miserable; I was not.

I was a most fortunate child. Ours was a home rich enough in family harmony and love to immunize eight kids against the potentially toxic effects of the environment beyond our door. Since the social scientists do not, as far as I know, have a clinical name for the fortunate possessors of this kind of emotional security, I might suggest they label them "the privileged poor." Poverty never succeeded in degrading our family. We were independently poor.

Our home was a battleground in the relentless struggle not only for survival (which even beasts can manage) but for survival with dignity. This was the American Revolution fourth floor back.

Mama and Papa were the leaders of this band of freedom fighters consisting of seven sons and one daughter, whose homemade weapons were hard work, family pride and, above all, faith in education as the major weapon of our liberation movement. Our watchword was a variant of the adage "Better to light a candle than curse the darkness." We did curse the darkness quite a bit, but we also lit candles, fires, lamps—and we studied by all of them.

Those were not the "good old days," but there were more victories than defeats, and each small victory was cause for a large celebration around the dinner table at the end of the day. Each member of the clan would recount his conquests at the shop or in school, with as much gesticulation as exaggeration, to the great delight of the others, who responded with much back-slapping, hysterical laughter and chants of victory. We became superb actors in an unfinished tragi-comedy called "The Battle Against Poverty." We tried by every device we could contrive to outwit the enemy—to outshout it, upstage it and confuse it by ad-libbing little pieces of business not in the script. We never played it the same way twice. Although we were not sure just how the play would end, we did have visions, not so much of a happy ending as of some happy new beginning in some special place of honor reserved for conquerors of poverty and its allies—disease and ignorance.

According to studies made by social-service agencies, a good home is defined as one in which there are love, acceptance, belonging, high moral standards, good parental example, decent food, clothing, shelter, spiritual guidance, discipline, joint enterprises, a place to bring friends, and respect for authority. Today any child, rich or poor, who lives in such a home is considered a "lucky kid." By these standards, then, I was a "lucky kid," not in spite of my home but because of it.

It is also possible—and this is not unusual among poor

children—that I went on my merry way being merry simply because I did not know any better. I had no idea, for instance, that I was entitled to a bed of my own. It was obvious even to an ordinary kid like me that the more kids you slept with the more fun you had in bed. I figured that was what they meant by "bedlam." I didn't know that beds were supposed to be soft. To me "bed and board" meant one and the same thing.

I didn't feel that privacy was especially desirable. What was attractive about being alone? I thought that going to the bathroom with a friend was real friendly. It transformed a biological necessity into a social amenity.

I didn't know that a long narrow street was not an ideal baseball diamond. I was so busy playing I didn't have time to check the measurements. The butcher store was first base, the sewer second, the laundry third, and the open manhole home plate. You slid in and down, and if you didn't waste your time foolishly while you were there you could find old baseballs.

I didn't know there were good cuts of meat and bad. Our menu at mealtime offered two choices—take it or leave it—an approach that seemed to stimulate our appetites. Most meat came to our table in the form of meatballs. (I had an idea that cows laid meatballs the way chickens lay eggs.) I didn't know that meatballs were supposed to contain meat. To this day I don't like the taste of meatballs made of meat. They just don't taste like Mama's.

I didn't know we were supposed to eat fresh bread. Mama said it would give us a bellyache; stale bread was much better for us. She believed so strongly in the stale-bread theory that she even learned to bake day-old bread.

Our block had about twenty tenements; each building about thirty families (not counting sleep-in strangers); each family about 5.6 children (not counting stowaways) by government census—if the census taker could halt the increase long enough to write down the number. There are towns in the United States with smaller populations which have a post office of their own. Yet I never felt crowded in or crowded out. My neighbors never appeared as a crowd to me. To the rich all poor people look alike. To me they were individuals—not all good and kind and noble, but individuals. We knew all about them and they all about us.

I didn't know I needed some quiet place where I could do my homework. My brothers used to sit around the dining-room table in the evening doing homework en masse, noisily, bothering each other, correcting, helping. They didn't know they were doing it all wrong. Tough luck! It's too late to rectify it now that they are educated and doing nicely. I didn't know I was supposed to be obsessed by sibling rivalries, so I admired my brothers and learned a great deal from them.

I didn't know mothers were supposed to use psychology on children. I knew they used whatever was immediately available, like shaving strops, wooden ladles, or the ever-ready palm of the hand which wise Mother Nature had shaped to fit perfectly over the rear end of a kid. Wise Mother Levenson simply applied wise Mother Nature's wisdom to us.

I didn't know that fathers were not supposed to hit kids if they were bad. Most fathers hit kids—anybody's.

The kid whose father didn't hit him felt that his father either wasn't interested in him or wasn't his real father. Besides, as any honest kid will tell you under oath, there are days when kids can be quite impossible—like Monday through Sunday, for instance. Come to think of it, the only perfect kid I ever heard of was my father when he was a kid.

I didn't know I had to *feel like* doing my homework, practicing the violin, washing dishes or running errands. I just *had* to do it because everyone had to do things he really didn't feel like doing—even big people. I had a strong suspicion my father didn't feel like working twelve hours a day in a sweatshop.

I learned from experience that if there was something lacking it might turn up if I went after it, saved up for it, worked for it, but never if I just waited for it. Of course, you had to be lucky, too, but I discovered that the more I hustled the luckier I seemed to get.

As an additional safeguard against self-pity in our home, Mama kept several charity boxes marked "For the Poor." We gave to the poor regularly. It made us feel rich.

Lest all this appear as a defense of the notion that ignorance is bliss, I'd like to tell you what I *did* know. I knew that there were things I wanted badly, things I would ask for. Mama's answer to such requests usually came in two words: "Not now." (Later we came to refer to this approach as Mama's theory of postponement of pleasure.) First things first. First came the absolute *necessities* like books. Skates, sleds and bicycles would have to wait. I know Mama didn't enjoy denying us the joys of childhood. She had to, in the interest of our adulthood.

"You'll have to do *without* today if you want a tomorrow *with*."

❁❁❁❁❁

Our parents set the moral tone of the family. They expected more of some of us and less of others, but never less than they thought we were capable of. "The Levensons"—Joe, Jack, Dora, David, Mike, Bill, Albert and Sammy—were different from each other, yet very much alike, as children and as adults. As brothers we were expected to collaborate rather than compete. Each was responsible not only to himself but to his brother, and all were responsible to our parents, who were prepared to answer to the world for all of us.

Mama and Papa hoped to derive joy from their children. "May you have joy from your children" was the greatest blessing conceivable. They were the parting words on happy and sad occasions. Honor brought to parents by their children was the accepted standard for measuring success. It also became an incentive for us. Our personal success was to a great extent predicated upon the happiness we could bring to our parents. It would not be long before this idea would be completely reversed. To make our children happy was to become the *summum bonum* of family life.

I should like to tell you how my brothers and sister turned out; then we can go back to the beginning of things.

As the children of immigrants my brothers were aware of the fact that they represented the "undesirables," the "foreigners," as others had been "undesirables" in previous decades. They realized, too, that the only way to rise above undesirability was not merely to become desirable, but to become indispensable. This would require equal amounts of education and sacrifice. They filled every hour not devoted to study with part-time jobs as truant officers, book salesmen, teachers of English to foreigners—wearing out their eyes, their pants and their books, drinking black coffee to stay awake, postponing marriage, sharing clothes, colds, money and dreams. They defined freedom as the opportunity to change the circumstances of your life through your own effort, to force the hand of history rather than to remain forever enslaved by it.

Joe, the eldest, became a doctor (Fordham, 1920). Jack, next in line, became a dentist (Columbia, 1924). They were the first to break through the barbed-wire fence of poverty. Because of them it was easier for the rest of us.

Through all the bleak years that Joe spent in medical school Papa could contribute nothing but a regular allowance of moral support. Joe will tell you to this day that he sews up a wound just like his father, the tailor, did. The stitches never show. He has still retained one nasty habit, though—he bites off the thread, a trick he learned from Mama who, in turn, learned a lot from Joe. He used to show her medical pictures of man's insides. "Just like a chicken," Mama observed. Joe will also tell you about the skull he brought home. The brothers placed it in the bookcase. At night they would put a lighted candle into it to scare off burglars. It worked. The one burglar who got in was so terrified he forgot his tools. We gave them to Joe, who used them on us, his first patients. (Joe told us years later that after he had explained human birth control to Papa, the only thing Papa asked was whether it could be retroactive.)

Jack, immediately after graduation from dental school, was besieged by all the moneyless tenants of our building, who provided him with the kind of professional experience money couldn't buy. After a while he learned how to cope with the situation. He either told them that nothing was wrong, or that they needed a specialist—my cousin Alvin.

Papa never quite forgave Mama for having broken his record by giving him a daughter. The other fathers on the block consoled Papa. After all, it happened while he was still young and hadn't hit his stride. Our only sister's name is Dora. To this day none of us can remember where she got dressed. She is the clearing house for all news, gossip, birth announcements and recipes. Dora has been the family historian, the curator of pictures, medals, legal documents, and old silver. She knows everybody's age but her own.

David was the Horatio Alger kid of our family. He had only one job in all his life. At the age of sixteen he went to work as a bookkeeper for a clothing jobber. He is now a partner in the business. He has not gone out to lunch in forty years. He can't make it because during lunch hour all the poor relatives come for suits.

Michael, next in line, threw Mama completely. At about the age of fourteen he won a medal for art. An artist in the family? "From this you expect to make a living? Learn a trade!" But there was no stopping him. He studied art all day and worked in the post office all night. Mama used to leave his portion of chopped liver on a plate so that he could have "a little something" before he went to bed. This unprotected delicacy standing on the table for hours brought out the wolf in the rest of us. Each one would wait till no one else was around, scoop out a little section of the liver, gulp it down, and flatten out the remainder with the palm of his hand so it would cover the same area. By the time Mike sat down to eat he could see the design on the plate through the liver.

To make matters worse, Michael refused to stay in commercial art where he could have made easy money. In the same cold bedroom where Joe had studied medicine and Jack dentistry, he painted in oils. We slept in a dense aroma of pigment and turpentine. He finally had to leave the house in order to make his struggle less painful to Mama and Papa.

At the age of twenty-three Michael Lenson (his nom de brush) won the Chaloner Prize which sent him to study in Europe for five years. The relatives sent him off with about thirty-two hand-knit sweaters and sixty-seven jars of homemade jelly. Newspaper photographers came and took pictures, and there was lots of crying and kidding. From Paris he sent me some of his prize money to buy a violin.

He worked at the Slade School, University of London, then went on to study and paint in France, Italy, Spain and the Netherlands, while exhibiting his work at the Goupil Gallery in London and in the Printemps and Automne salons in Paris. In subsequent years he has shown in such group shows as the Carnegie International, Corcoran Gallery, Museum of Modern Art, Pennsylvania Academy, Albright Gallery, Butler Institute, Art USA, and the Cleveland, Rochester, Dallas, and Newark museums, to name a few. As art critic, he is now in his eleventh year with the Newark *Sunday News*.

In reviewing his last one-man show, one of the critics said: "His art is projected as a moral force . . . wherein content must serve as the vehicle for human values." This, I suspect, he learned at home before he went to Paris. His life has remained unfulfilled in only one respect—he still can't get enough chopped liver.

Bill, next in line, became a successful dental technician. At first he decided not to work for somebody else for ten hours a day—not him, boy—so he went into business and worked twelve hours a day—for himself, boy. After about forty years of this kind of "independence" he decided to work eight hours a day for somebody who works twelve hours a day. Bill, the kindest, gentlest, and most devoted to the family, died on July 3, 1965. Our magic number has been reduced forever. We are now eight minus one. It will never be the same without that one.

Albert, just ahead of me, has been at my side all my life. He had a genius for getting into trouble. He did not go looking for it. He didn't have to. It came looking for him. Somehow he was always available.

I was there when:

1. The revolving door at the Automat jammed on Albert when he was halfway through. In the presence of hundreds of people studying Albert under glass, a crew of mechanics had to release him.

2. Albert took two steps on the sidewalk to let an elderly man pass, and found himself in a cellar with a freshly delivered ton of coal for company.

3. Albert walked into the house carrying a jar of sour cream. He slipped on the freshly washed wooden planks and the jar hit the floor. Normally the cream would splash on the floor, but not for Albert. The jar hit the floor and the cream hit the ceiling. This may not work for you even if you try it, but for Albert this was a "natural."

Through all his disasters Albert was silent. Even as a child he never cried. It drove Mama mad. She would shake him. "Cry, for God's sake, cry."

He has been my librarian and secretary for years. His remarkable memory provided much of the documentation of this book.

I am the kid brother of the family. To this day when the boys get together they send me for ice cream, and I have to go. (Joe still calls me the "go-getter.") As the last of so many I presented a special problem to Mama, who in moments of anger often couldn't remember my name. She would stare at me and call off every name but mine: "Joe, no, Jack, no . . ." Out of sheer frustration, she would hit me. "You, what's your name?"

I became a schoolteacher and married Esther, who had waited eight years for me to get a job. It was customary at the time to get a job first, then a wife. I never claimed my college diploma. It cost $1.87. My cap-and-gown graduation picture is a further commentary on those days. Across the face are stamped the words "Proof Only."

All turned out to be quite remarkable adults. Aside from the fact that a couple of them made it into various Who's Whos, they are concertgoers, art patrons, theatergoers, book readers; they are keenly interested in their fellow man; they react strongly against social injustice. They are civilized people.

Now that we are all married (Joe to Kate; Jack to Florence; David to Elizabeth; Mike to June, Bill to Frieda; Albert to Helen; me to Esther; and Dora, most unfortunately widowed twice in her lifetime, to Sam and to Morris) and have families of our own, we often recall and try to assess the childhood experiences that experts tell us must have been traumatic. By current standards we were raised all wrong. Why, then, do we remember our parents' homes with affection? Did our parents have a method of raising children or was it merely trial and error? What were their values? Is the current crop of children happier than we were? Will they speak as well of us as we speak of our parents? What was it they gave us, they who said they had nothing to give?

The stories that follow may provide some of the answers.

Oᴜʀꜱ ᴡᴀꜱ ᴀ ʟɪꜰᴇ of plenty: plenty of relatives, neighbors, boarders, janitors, landlords, holidays, cockroaches, cats, dogs, music, books, romance, fights, parties, weddings, medals, illnesses, politicians, superstitions and junk.

According to the Constitution we were first-class citizens, but we could afford only second-class merchandise. We ate for years from a set of dairy dishes on the back of which were imprinted the words "U.S. Coast Guard Imperfect." Our neighborhood was the wastebasket of the city. We were the heirs to the shopworn, frayed, faded and castoff goods of our more affluent fellow Americans. Our household furnishings came from the poor man's antique shop, the slightly-used-as-good-as-new bargain store where we could bid on wares which were in the same fix we were.

The sign on the store window read ꜰᴜʀɴɪᴛᴜʀᴇ, but that covered only two brass beds, a chest of drawers and a kitchen table. The rest of the merchandise consisted of accessories for gracious living such as chipped punch glasses, bronze statues of Atlas holding up an ashtray, or a bell for calling the maid.

In front of the store there stood a bushel basket full of butter-dish covers and a book rack displaying books that the owner had found in the drawers of discarded furniture. For five cents per copy anyone with a thirst for learning could start a fine basic library containing *Lives of the Mexican Generals, Chrestomathie de la Poésie*

Turcque, Six Unaccompanied Sonatas for Bass Viol, Attributed to a Pupil of Monteverdi, The Practice of Insect Extermination, Second Edition, Letters of Admiral Breckenridge to His Nephew, and *How to Heat an Igloo.*

Our neighborhood also had an open-air pushcart market where there were genuine bargains: overripe onions, frost-bitten tomatoes, and a great variety of canned goods whose labels were burnt or missing. We called them "surprise lunches." There were large barrels of pickles (the best, as any good shopper could tell you, were always on the bottom), and even larger barrels full of bright-eyed herrings living in crowded quarters with their sisters, their cousins, their uncles and their aunts just as we did; tail ends of sturgeon, the meatier parts of which had been promoted to better neighborhoods; suits of long winter underwear suspended from high poles like effigies; and hoisted way above all was the flag of the pushcart fleet— pink bloomers full-blown in the wind. You could not try on underthings but you could buy them with the understanding that if they didn't fit after you got them home your money would be cheerfully refunded. The quality was guaranteed verbally: "It will last a lifetime, and after that you can make a skirt out of it." You could also buy tarnished crucifixes and Stars of David impiously displayed alongside trusses, hot-water bags, and remedies for the itch.

In this market you might latch onto a "reject"—a brand-new item with a birth defect. If the damage was in the back where it didn't show, you paid more than if it was in the front. After all, only you would know about the hidden damage, and you could keep a secret.

At twilight the human scavengers would descend upon

the market to buy up the marked down from the marked down, the foods that had been squeezed, bent, smelled and rejected. Hungry kids would never know the difference.

At the very end of a winter's day, when the peddlers were stiff with the cold, zero hour transactions such as the following were not unusual.

Lady, examining one last, tarnished teaspoon on a pushcart:

"How much?"

"A penny."

"Too much."

"Make me an offer."

In those days people did not live as long as they do today, but things lived longer. In our house old things were not discarded but retired to a drawer in the kitchen which we called "Mama's shame-to-throw-out drawer." Every family had one. It contained at all times such indispensables as half a pair of scissors, a toothless comb, eyeglass frames without lenses, empty Vaseline jars, a knotted rubber band, the face of a clock, a black button marked "Off," the bulb of a nasal spray, a fountain-pen tube, a ball of tinfoil, a key to the old apartment, and a "gold" medal which read "Best Wishes Thom McAn Shoes."

The drawer was appropriately lined with old newspaper, of which there was always a great abundance, since news, too, did not have to be new to be good. Mama saw no reason for buying new news when she had not yet used up the old.

Newspapers, in fact, served many functions besides covering the news; they also covered the floors, for instance. After the lady of the house had washed her wooden floors she covered them with newspaper, wall to wall. Many a time I came home from school to find Mama stretched out on the floor absorbed in an editorial.

The rotogravure section was reserved for sideboard-drawer lining because its brownish-red color matched our genuine imitation mahogany. The bottom drawer was known as the Maternity Ward. When our cat was expecting (again), Mama shredded a newspaper with her meat chopper and padded the drawer. Women understood such things. At our house kittens could read before they could walk.

I inherited most of my hats from older brothers, uncles and forgetful strangers, who got them that way themselves. The size was reduced to fit my head by folding a string of newspaper under the inside leather band.

Party hats were fashioned of cleverly folded newspaper, as were generals' hats, Chinese hats, chefs' hats, kings' crowns, sailboats, bandits' masks, megaphones, telescopes and fly-swatters.

A short, hand-rolled wad of newspaper served as a cork for bottles as well as a packing for keyholes when privacy was desired. (Keyholes were for looking, not for locking.)

We cut our schoolbook covers out of newspaper. My brother Mike could work it out so that an inspiring picture of Tom Mix's horse would appear smack on the front of the book.

Children were punished by being slapped on the head with a rolled-up newspaper. I must say, though, that no father was cruel enough to swat a kid with the Sunday paper. This might leave him punchy through the following Thursday.

Mama and my sister Dora cut newspapers into dress patterns—for fancy dresses the society page, for daily wear the Situations Wanted.

If any parts of the newspaper survived they were stored in the cellar for months. Eventually they were sold to the junk dealer who then sold the lot to the newspaper publisher whose mother probably had lots of floors to cover.

⁂

While we did not possess the purchasing power to buy first-class merchandise, we did possess the will power to be first-class human beings. Things could become junk, but people didn't have to accept such a fate. Man could fight back. A teapot, Mama said, had no soul, but man did.

Mama had a philosopher's insight and a prophet's foresight. She foresaw the corrupting effect of vermin not only on beds but on people in the beds, the gnawing of rats not only on plaster but on the moral fiber of humans. Dirt is bad company. Dirty beds could breed dirty thoughts which could breed dirty deeds.

Mama, therefore, practiced preventive housekeeping. Capitulation to a second-class physical environment might mean the renunciation of first-class ideals. Personal honor, behavior and character could never be "marked down." Mama's search for defects in the quality of our values was far more exacting than her appraisal of a pushcart bargain. She made it pretty clear that our home was not a pushcart, and that our integrity would not be reduced. Mama insisted that we were a first-class family, and that among the few treasures she could afford in life was a clean home.

Her fight against dirt was based upon the premise that circumstance makes poor, but people make dirt, and that if everyone cleaned his own house inside and out, the whole world would be clean. If Mama had to contend with the environment, the environment would have to contend with Mama. She was the environment's problem.

Some housekeepers threw in the mop: "You want dirt? I'll show you dirt!" Mama reacted with spite. "You want dirt? Not from me. I'll show you who's boss in this house! I'll show you clean like you never saw clean. I'll kill you with cleanliness." She did, in fact, almost kill my brother Albert, who ran through a closed window onto the fire escape to watch a parade going by. Mrs. Clean had polished the window to the point where it was invisible. The day Mrs. Gordon, upstairs, forgot to clean her windows Mama was quick to remark, "Next thing you know she'll start using lipstick."

Today psychiatrists would call Mama a compulsive housekeeper. She would get up at 6 A.M. mumbling, "Here it is Monday, before you know it Tuesday, and Wednesday just around the corner, and Thursday running into Friday, and I haven't done a stitch of work yet."

Bedmaking in our house began earlier than in most, and more suddenly. It started with either three or four of us on the bedroom floor, depending on which bed Mama overturned first. If we didn't come to quickly enough we often found ourselves folded up in a mattress on the fire escape. Or Mama would pretend to be considerate. She wouldn't wake you. "You want to sleep? Sleep. Sleep. Sleep." And she would pull the sheet out from under you, start pounding the pillows with a carpet beater, and proceed to make the bed with you in it.

One morning I was sent home by my teacher: "Young man, you look sick. Go right home and tell your mother to put you to bed." I walked into the house to find Mama in her customary position—on her knees, wet rag in hand, next to a pail of sudsy-gray water. "The teacher said I'm sick and that I should lie down in bed."

Mama looked up. "In what? Are you sure you can't sit up? I just made the bed!"

Mama would sooner have been caught drunk than have anyone, especially a stranger, walk in and find her house dirty. My brothers used to joke about it: "Mama's ashamed to leave dirty dishes in the sink overnight. If a burglar broke in she would be embarrassed."

At our house "The line is busy" meant that Mama was hanging out the wash. On Monday at dawn you were wakened by the twittering of hysterical sparrows trying to reply to the squealing of the clothesline pulleys. By noon all the women had hung their laundry. All light was shut out of the yard by the hundreds of garments crisscrossing each other to form an impenetrable forest of wet wash.

In that yard I picked up a working knowledge of sex. By studying the wash, I could determine whether Mrs. Burns's daughters were now "big girls" by the appearance of brassieres and panties, or whether they were still "little girls" who wore woolen bloomers.

My mother had an all-male line of "union suits"

(closed shop but for the trap door), with the exception of her own long nightgowns which hung down two full flights when they were wet, and my sister Dora's skirts which dripped in technicolor onto other people's white laundry.

My job on Mondays was to "run down into the yard and pick up the handkerchiefs that fell off the line before someone takes them." The reason I didn't like to go was that some window would invariably fly open and an angry woman would call down to me, "What are you doing there?"

"I'm picking up my mother's handkerchiefs."

"They're mine, not your mother's." Other windows would open. The battle was on.

"They're not his and they're not yours. They're mine."

"And how do you know they're yours?"

"If I don't know mine who knows mine?"

"And I know mine."

"May I not live to see my daughter married if it's not mine."

"Don't swear for a handkerchief. It doesn't pay. It's not a tablecloth."

It would take days before peace was restored.

The difference between keeping things clean and keeping kids clean was that things just sat still and waited for the dirt to collect. We kids were carriers. We ran a pickup and delivery service.

If you brought dirt into the house your name was mud. A kangaroo court was in session at all times. Mama would line up the eight kids against the kitchen wall, one hand pointing at us accusingly, the other pointing up to the evidence: the mark of a rubber ball on the ceiling. What she said does not seem to make much sense now, but it did then. "I just scrubbed that ceiling on my hands and knees and now look. Who did it?"

Sometimes when we walked into the house we would get a wet rag square in the face for two reasons: one, to clean; two, to identify. "Let me see which slob it is." Mama sometimes cleaned off the grimy little faces of total strangers. "You I don't know. Out!"

If Mama didn't happen to have a rag in her hand she wiped your face with the edge of her apron which she had moistened with *your* spit. "Here, spit on this." Obviously she knew it was unsanitary for us to use other people's spit.

It wasn't that we kids loved dirt; we simply valued time more. Keeping clean used up too much of a kid's valuable minutes. There was so much to do. There was ink to be spilled, chalk to be stepped on, toothpaste to be squirted, pencil shavings to be scattered, and windows to be fingerprinted.

It's hard to believe that dirt could overcome hunger, but it did.

"Ma, I'm hungry."

"Wash your hands; I'll give you a piece of bread and butter."

"I'm not hungry."

One of Mama's favorite teaching techniques was comparison—impossible us versus some paragon of elegance. "Does President Coolidge hang his dirty socks on a doorknob? Answer me! Does Rudolph Valentino leave his sneakers on his bed? Answer me! Does Chaim Weizmann chew his tie? Does the Prince of Wales throw newspaper into his mother's toilet bowl?"

When all else failed Mama made the announcement that put fear in our hearts. "All right; enough is enough. Tomorrow the Board of Health is coming to take you all away. Goodbye."

Came Monday morning however, you wouldn't have recognized us. We had to be thoroughly clean, even where it didn't show, like inside the ears "you shouldn't give me any excuses that you didn't hear what the teacher said." Our hands had to be scrubbed clean as a surgeon's notwithstanding brother Albert's claim that "I never raise my hand in class, anyhow." In school it was essential not only to spell good, but to smell good. You even had to put on a fresh, clean shirt. On lesser occasions, if you got caught putting on a clean shirt Mama would say, "Take it off before you get it dirty."

For school we had to take a bath. "Scratching, like borrowing, helps only for a while," Mama said. We reluctantly turned in our bodies to Mama and submitted to Operation Skin Removal. We resisted, connived, lied, and finally ran out of effective evasions. "It's not dirt; it's my tan from last summer" had been used too often, as had "It's too soon after my cold." We made token attempts at cleanliness by following the spray truck on the street, rubbing our faces and arms in the muddy mist it left in its wake. We walked in the rain face up. Before putting on a fresh shirt we determined whether it had long sleeves or short, and washed ourselves accordingly.

Any one of us who of his own free will just went and took a bath (like brother David who was unnaturally neat for a child) had a lot of explaining to do. "What's the matter you're taking a bath, you going to the doctor or something?"

We knew about cleanliness being next to Godliness, but taking a bath in our home was next to impossible. For six days a week our bathtub served as a storage bin for paint cans, brushes, wine jugs, umbrellas, toilet plungers, soiled laundry and a day-to-day supply of coal. Before we could be bathed, the tub had to be scoured and the bathroom sealed off. There was a broken window over the bathtub, which had never been replaced. We covered it with a board that the boys referred to as the "draft board." Since there was never a supply of water hot enough to deterge urgent cases like ours, steaming reinforcements were brought to the scene in teakettles, pots and pans. After Mama had made the elbow test (if the skin blistered it was just right), we were thrown in en masse to soak, like laundry. Since the stopper was always missing, we seated a soft, fat brother at the drain end.

Mama washed kids like she washed floors. She tore through our scalps with a horse brush soaked in naphtha soap. We screamed in pain as the acids ate into every aperture. To kill the lice she added kerosene. "Please, Ma! Enough!" Not yet. Her fingers dug into both your ears, twisting, turning, brain-washing mercilessly. You were left draped over the rim of the tub in a state of amnesia, recognizing nobody, frothing at the mouth, promising to be a good boy in the future, ready to sign any confession.

This fierce bathing ritual was another expression of Mama's constant battle against the environment. As I lay in my clean bed recovering from the ordeal by water I knew the great joy of pride in one's body. My self-esteem had been lifted. I felt important, fresh, redeemed. I was glad to be alive and very much in love with the world and my home. The sin of dirt which the street had inflicted upon me had been washed away, and I was reborn, a first-class citizen, the equal of any kid.

Years later, the older boys, who were beginning to earn money, hired a woman to come once a week to help Mama. On the day she was due, Mama got up at five-thirty, scrubbed the floors and put up fresh curtains, "Nobody should think we're pigs." When the lady arrived, Mama had hot coffee ready for her. They compared aches and pains, including a few heartaches, recipes, husbands, children and blood pressures. When she left they cried on each other's shoulders, and Mama promised to come and help her with her house real soon.

※※※※※

When Papa married Mama he put a ring on one of her fingers and thimbles on all the others. Without benefit of bifocals she could thread a needle in the dark with one hand, tie a knot with her teeth, and chop meat with her free hand. She pumped away at her sewing machine like a six-day bicycle rider, used up enough energy to go around the world three times, and never left home.

Long pants were belittled into short pants; old skirts became new aprons; old aprons became good as new collars; collars were reversed and re-reversed; sleeves were amputated to the elbow; cuffs were successfully transplanted and grafted onto strange pants—and the scar never showed. All garments, outer or under, public or private,

mentionable or unmentionable, could be made to fit anyone. "Use it up, wear it out; make it do or do without."
If your sleeves were short you got longer mittens. Padding
the size of beanbags took care of sloping shoulders, and
flour sacks expanded the crotches of narrow-minded under-
shorts. Besides, whatever Mama Levenson couldn't fill in,
Father Time would: "He'll grow into it." Mama was not
concerned with fashion but with nakedness. "It's good
enough for now." We were never sure how long now
would be.

Clothing was always en route from one kid to another.
Typical conversations ran something like this:

"Ma, where's my shirt?"

"Which shirt?"

"The one that used to be Albert's jumper that used to
be Jack's sport shirt that used to be Dora's blouse."

"Oh, that one? Too late. It's Albert's underwear now."

Mama hated holes the way nature abhors a vacuum. A
rip was followed immediately by a patch. The colors of
her patches were brilliant, and no two were alike. When
brother Bill bent over, he looked like a stained-glass window.

Mama cut up the oldest blankets to patch the older
ones. The old blankets were not even used. They were
considered too new to be put on the beds.

Even a hole in the head was covered with a patch, not
necessarily white, and certainly not sterile, but effective.
The germs died of overpopulation.

The knot was a handy device for tying off poverty. If
one of us kids tore his shoelace, he didn't pull out the
remainder and discard it. It was cheaper to make a knot
and lace the shoe only three-quarters of the way up. After

the next break came more knots. The lace usually ended up outlasting the shoe.

If the top button of your shorts tore off you could pull the section where the button had been through the button-hole, then tie a knot into it, and it would hold better than a button.

Between the hours of after supper and bedtime Mama could always be found knitting things for the family, "Here, hold out your hands." I would hold taut a skein of wool while she rolled it into a ball. She was off on a new project. Often there were mystery knittings. "A surprise for you; something you need." This was no help at all because I needed everything. It never fit the one for whom it was intended, but there were so many of us that it was bound to fit at least one.

The whole family watched in fascination as the thing began to take form. When I saw it had no fingers, I decided it was a mitten. When she left off the thumb, I decided it was a hat. When she left off the woolly knob on top, I decided it was socks after all, especially because she had measured my hand. Mama operated on the well-known scientific fact that the circumference of the fist is equal to the length of the foot. The socks Mama knitted had a heavy inner seam. It felt like walking barefoot on the blade of an ice skate. If we complained she would say, "They don't appreciate anything."

❁❁❁❁❁

Our flat was lit by gaslight. It always happened that when we had company the gas flame would begin to sputter and fade, a deliberate attempt on the part of the public utilities to embarrass us. We would hold a tribal council. Brother Joe would be hoisted up to examine the delicate gauze mantle. The slightest twitch of the hand, and it would crumble into a fine gray ash, and the slightest twitch did not fail to materialize. The problem was now half solved. We could prove we had a broken mantle on our hands.

We now had to face the possibility that we were also out of gas. We never accepted this alternative until we had tried to massage the heart of the gas meter. It trembled a bit, but still no heartbeat. The meter had lots of clocks and indicators and numbers. We rotated the knobs like safecrackers, fingered the dials, tried mouth-to-mouth resuscitation by blowing into the coin slot, poked toothpicks into every opening. We tried every known method of revivification short of depositing a quarter, hoping for the miracle of the tenement—light without money.

Now that enough time has elapsed for our family to be immune from prosecution I can confess that sometimes these tricks worked. We could prolong the life of a meter by two or three days. We don't know how it happened, but on one occasion my brother Bill, who had developed strong fingers from tuning his ukulele, forced a dial to the point where we not only had free gas for a month, but got a refund from the company.

Electricity didn't come into our house until we were all grown up. Even then we were restricted to only essential use of the electric lights. If you threw the switch for some silly reason such as to see where you were going, Papa would appear out of the shadows with a "Hello, Mr. Rockefeller." A light on all night meant somebody was in trouble. "Let him have the bulb; he's sick." Under the best of conditions no bulb was ever more than twenty-five watts. Public Futilities, Jack called them.

❀❀❀❀❀

In many ways our flat anticipated the "Automatic Home of Tomorrow" one reads about in the magazines. We had a "deep-freeze" unit directly outside the kitchen window —with real snow on it. It defrosted itself automatically each spring.

The kitchen sink had "swing-easy" faucets which swung round and round and finally came off in your hand. Nearly all faucets were optimistically marked "Hot." We could tell the difference by watching them drip: the "Cold" dripped warm and the "Hot" dripped rusty. On winter days the cold wind came up through the Hot faucet.

There was "indirect lighting" from the street lamp outside. The problem of kitchen odors was solved by "exhaust ventilation" via a "recessed" hole in the ceiling that heated the "sunken living room" of the apartment upstairs.

Cabinet doors were operated by "remote control." If you banged the front door the dish closet in the kitchen ejected a shelf of ready-cracked dishes. We had automatic dishwashers, too. In those days they were called children.

Our kitchen table would today be called "functional" or "multipurpose." On the same table where the brothers did homework, Mama rolled dough (many a missing report card turned up in a spongecake), Dora ironed laundry, Jack cut up frogs, and Mike practiced handstands. Man! That's togetherness! (It was Mike's handstands that ultimately created a "drop leaf" at the end of the table.)

By placing an ironing board across two chairs you could

seat and feed four dinner guests. If the company stayed over, the very same "miracle table" could be expanded by inserting enough boards to sleep four people comfortably.

In addition to rooms each of which was approximately the size and shape of a closet, we had a "walk-in closet" next to the door to our apartment. The boys called it the "good-night closet." Departing guests used to say politely "Good night" and politely walk into the closet.

When one of the boys showed Mama her first magazine picture of a real modern streamlined kitchen she said, "God forbid. It looks like a hospital."

Several pieces of furniture stand out in my memory. There was an item common to the era known as the "lounge," a cross between a bed of nails, an examination table and a psychiatrist's couch. In the summer it sweated by itself. If you took a nap on it in mid-afternoon you had to be peeled off like a Band-Aid.

Our bureau had knobs all over. Most of them were purely decorative, but the real ones were easy to detect; they came out when you pulled them. It had three drawers. The handles for the top drawer had been removed and placed in the bottom drawer so they wouldn't get lost. You couldn't get at the bottom drawer, except through the middle drawer. The handles for the middle drawer were in the top drawer. The top drawer could only be opened with a crowbar, which is why we called it the "breakfront." Once you had the top drawer out, you put in your hands and forced out the middle drawer, then stuck your hands into where the middle drawer had been and forced out the bottom drawer where you found the knobs to the top drawer. If one of us asked Papa for a penny he would say, "Look in the middle drawer." That would keep us busy for an afternoon.

There was also a china closet, which originally had sharp edges that Papa had rounded off in the process of scratching his back against them. This china closet contained the "good dishes" which were used only if "people" came. The immediate family was not "people." When we moved, the "good dishes" were placed on top of the barrels for "people" to see.

Every family had a wooden icebox in the kitchen. Many of these were quite handsome, with elaborate carving; some were even topped with a mirror.

According to the geologists the ice age ended thousands of years ago—except in our home, where Mama kept it alive for years. It ended officially only after we threw out our icebox. My mother could keep a piece of ice going for weeks. She managed this by various methods.

1. Unless an emergency develops, don't open the icebox. Opening causes melting, and melting is not healthy for ice. (To this day, when I open the refrigerator door I expect to hear a voice say, "Close the icebox.")

2. Never put food into the icebox. Food will also melt the ice. The best place for food is outside the window.

There were several ways of transporting ice from the ice docks to our house.

1. *The old baby carriage.* You placed the ice where the baby would normally sit and covered it with a warm blanket to protect it from the sun's rays and life's hard knocks.

2. *The homemade wagon.* This was an old fruit box nailed onto a shaft, which traveled either on a pair of

broken-down roller skates or a set of wobbly spoke-impoverished wheels.

3. *The rope method.* You tied a piece of rope around the cake of ice and dragged same over the sidewalks. We were expert at the art of gently sliding the ice from the sidewalk into the gutter and up again without cracking it. Sometimes pieces did break off in spite of our best efforts. We brought the detached chunks home in our pockets or carried them under our armpits until it became too painful. Little chips were ours to enjoy. You put them into your mouth and sucked them. If you managed to get the ice home safely, all you got was a scolding for bringing such a small piece. "Send an infant for something . . ."

‡‡‡‡‡

"It is not good for man to be alone," Papa used to say, quoting from the *Poor Man's Almanac of Rationalizations* —so we slept in various sets: four in a bed (the group plan); three in a bed (semiprivate, unless one of the three had a contagious disease, in which case he was allowed to sleep with only one, preferably one who had never had the disease); two in a bed (doubleheader); and one in a bed (critical list). Hopeless cases slept in Mama's bed. Chairs and floors also served as beds. Floors were preferred because you could not fall off.

In order to insure a reasonable amount of air not already filtered through our bed partner's adenoids, we slept not tête-à-tête but foot-à-tête—cross-ventilation we called it—an arrangement that made it impossible to cough into a brother's face; we could cough only into his feet.

There were other sleeping patterns such as crisscross, ticktacktoe, checkerboard, pyramids and shambles. A sudden sneeze by the kid in the middle of any of these configurations could trigger a chain reaction which sent kids flying in all directions.

The procedure of getting bedded down for the night often started with the shock treatment. Just before bedtime Mama would reel in the clothesline, remove several sheets of ice which earlier in the day had been sheets of linen, put them on your bed and say, "Go to bed." Those were the nights when nobody fought to be first in bed. Mama would reduce the intensity of the shock by placing a hot stove lid wrapped in a towel at your feet. I still carry the name of the stove manufacturer branded on my left arch.

Some people brag that they sleep like a rock. I slept *on* one. Mama's pillows were about the size of a home movie screen and were as hard as bags of cement. You slept with your head propped up as though you were lying in state. Years later, as we got married, Mama made each of us a present of a set of pillows extracted from the mother pillow. Still, no matter how much stuffing Mama pulled out of the original, it never got softer.

For most people, sound sleep implies quiet. We slept through the sounds of a world that never slept. Our nervous systems were geared to noise. Silence would have shocked us. We slept through the din of fire engines, trolleys, trucks, trains, slamming doors, barking dogs and wailing cats. Within our own walls plumbing hummed, faucets chirped, bedsprings twanged, stoves hissed, mattresses groaned, floors creaked, windows banged, and the window shades wildly applauded all the performances.

While there was room for all to sleep, quilts were at a premium, as were brothers with warm feet. The latter sold high on the open market. Deals for quilts were made before bedtime. We called it the Cover Charge. "Hey, Al! If you let me have the heavy quilt tonight I'll give you my searchlight for lend for two days." The heavy quilt was not warm, just heavy, but therein lay its merit. It didn't slide off the bed. It rested there like a mound of earth on a fresh grave, and we slept the sleep of the just. That quilt could cover three of us, if one of us were not my brother Mike, who was not just a restless sleeper—he was a night crawler. He would start moving across the bed on a forty-five degree angle from the footboard to the headboard, instinctively dragging the quilt along his route. We held on for dear life and he dragged us, quilt and all, wherever he was going. The tug-of-war lasted until we all fell asleep from sheer exhaustion.

Papa's heavy coat was a prize. He had brought it from the old, cold country and it was lined with fur. We would slip our feet through the sleeves, button ourselves into the hairy straitjacket and hibernate for one winter's night at a time.

The coldest room in the house was the front room. To get any warmth into it you would have had to open the windows. Mama used to keep her marinated fish there. In order to survive the night in that room you wore a sweater under your undershirt, and long woolen socks. But Mother Nature, not nearly so kind as our own mother, had a way of taunting us on extra-cold nights. Just when you were nice and warm, the call came. You tried to throw her off your track by concentrating on deserts, droughts, sand dunes or petrified forests—all to no avail.

"Hey, Al. Come with me. It's dark." It was not the dark alone I was afraid of. There was the ghoulish red face of the hot coal stove and, even more frightening, the phosphorescent glow of Mama's teeth in a glass in the kitchen.

Al wouldn't come. "Not me, buddy."

"I'll give you my searchlight for lend for *three* days."

"Make it a week."

"O.K. If you throw in the heavy quilt."

"It's a deal."

Together we made the trip to the toilet dragging the bartered quilt after us lest some older brother roll up in it and claim seniority rights.

Talking about toilets may not be in the best of taste, but neither was living in a tenement with a toilet in the yard. (Brother David referred back to it years later as our Cabana Club.) The words "Ma, throw me down the key" or "Ma, we're out of orange wrappers" have a very special connotation to the alumni of the tenements.

A night call might require a hike down five flights of stairs in your underwear, struggling all the while to retain your dignity, your sleep, and whatever it was you were retaining. Some tenement dwellers kept a chamberpot under their beds, usually part of a set referred to by tenement wits as a "baseball set—a pitcher on the bureau and a catcher under the bed." Rich people also owned these sets, but theirs were porcelain. In our building the chamber was usually a zinc pail which, when used on a crisp, cold night, could create the effect of a whining fire-engine siren. Wise guys used to open the window and yell, "Where's the fire?"

※※※※※

Our family and the landlord had only one thing in common—we were both trying to raise the rent. If we ever paid him on the first of the month he would say, "What's this? Paying in advance?" It must be said on his behalf that he never hounded us. He used the oblique method. If the rent was late, he would appear at about 6 A.M. in the company of a strange woman and show the apartment, ignoring us as completely as though we were spirits visible only to each other, while we stood there in our patched underwear too ashamed and frightened to protest that we were human and alive.

The cold war between tenants and landlords conditioned our thinking so deeply that if even the youngest among us had been given an association test and the word "landlord" were mentioned, we would automatically have responded with "that crook." I don't recall ever hearing him referred to merely as "the landlord." His title was always qualified by such denunciations as "that bloodsucker," "that leech," "that beast." Our attitude toward each other was based upon the dialectics of class distrust. We said we were making him rich; he said we were making him poor.

Perhaps he particularly disliked our clan because we had deceived him. Finding an apartment for a family our size wasn't easy. When our parents went looking for a place to live they took along only two of the children.

The day we moved in, the landlord stood in the doorway transfixed watching eight kids scramble off the moving van. His face turned white immediately, his hair just a few seconds later. He looked at Mama, and in a voice choked by a mixture of paternal interest and vested interest said, "Why didn't you tell me you had such a beautiful family?" And Mama, understanding his ambivalence, said, "I didn't have the heart."

The day after we moved in, the landlord made an offer that seemed to appeal to Papa: "Eight children is too many. I'll take only two." And Papa countered with "It's a deal. Which two do you want?"

The landlord seemed civil enough at first. He told Mama not to hesitate to report any problem. "Above all, don't worry, Mrs. Levenson." When Mama told the landlord the sink was going to fall right through the floor, he said, "Don't worry. Let the people downstairs worry."

He could have said No to all of Mama's requests but he never did.

"You promised Mrs. Hessel a new stove."

"O.K. So I'll promise you one, too."

If he promised one tenant a new stove and the others heard about it, nobody got a new stove. When our doorbell stopped working he remedied that by taking our name out of the letter box.

If, as he said, he couldn't be bothered with small repairs, we could give him big ones. A small hole in the wall could easily be made large enough for a landlord to walk through.

"Mrs. Levenson," he said, "I'm a landlord who likes happy tenants. If you are not happy, please move." And

Mama came up with the ultimate in ultimata: "Either you paint or we stay." His reply was: "Why should I put myself out? I'd rather put you out!"

At one point in our stormy coexistence his attitude changed. He "Good morning'd" and "How are you'd" all over the place. Then it came out—he had sold the house.

∞∞∞∞∞

The janitor, as poor if not poorer than the rest of us, suffered from guilt by association. He represented *him*. He was the devil's disciple, and like the devil, he lived near the flames of the furnace in the nether regions of the building, amidst coal and ashes. He was followed always by a vicious dog and a bird that talked in a foreign tongue.

He cursed his way through his onerous duties, trying to repair the irreparable, vainly bandaging the oozing wounds of a house whose innards were hanging out all over, stemming perennial floods from sewers and roofs, splicing fractured banisters, polishing corroded brass, only to find himself submerged each morning by a fresh accumulation of tenement fallout.

We kids did very little to make life more bearable for that poor man. We would congregate on our stoop, which was decorated like the walls of ancient caves with native art: chalk drawings of our natural enemy, the janitor, squares for playing potsy, arithmetic examples, nude figures with fat bellies, dirty words, usually misspelled but close enough to deliver the message.

The stoop served as an information center for strangers

visiting the building. "Mrs. Berlin? Second floor front. Mrs. Kramer went to her sister in Brooklyn. Hessel? You can't go in there. They've got the measles."

Just as some big people were quick to say, "Go back where you came from," we kids practiced stoop chauvinism, chasing kids from other buildings who came to play on our stoop. "Go back to your own stoop! You don't belong here!"

Sometimes the rain would come and break up our stoop games. We would huddle in the hallway, that is, all of us but Nutty Louie, who waited for days like this to sail matchsticks in the gutter. He would sit on the curb, the rain streaming down his face, dreaming of ships that go down to the sea. His vessels went down the sewer, but undaunted he sent out new ones to ride the rapids over and around the garbage.

If the rainfall was heavy we would extend our dirty hands to catch and drink the warm liquid or rub it into our hair. "It's healthy."

We finger-painted designs and slogans on the steam that gathered on the big glass door of the hallway: "Nancy loves Irving." And Nancy would add an embarrassed postscript: "She does not."

The janitor would appear at regular intervals brandishing a broom and yelling, "Get out of the hall, you dirty bums." One brave soul would stand up to him with "My father pays taxes," and the rest of us, encouraged by his heroism, backed him up with a collective "Yeh." It felt good to have the Federal Government behind you. Nevertheless, we made a strategic withdrawal to the staircase leading to the cellar, where we then organized a "show."

The timid ones would sit on the wet stairs in tiers while the extroverts would sing the popular tunes of the day: "Barney Google, with His Goo-Goo-Googly-Eyes," "The Sheik of Araby," or "K-K-K-Katy, Beautiful Katy." Georgie entertained by exhibiting his missing finger. Harold sucked in his cheeks and made his eyes protrude, to everyone's delight. Henry kept his feet still and turned completely around to prove he was double-jointed. Great ovation. The show was called off when Nutty Louie ran in from the street to announce a spectacular. "Hey, fellers, a rainbow!"

∞∞∞∞∞

Mama's philosophy of live and let live did not include bedbugs and cockroaches, those vicious marauders that struck out at us in the night. We fought back in self-defense. We literally "stamped" them out with our heels. There was a popular two-step we called the cockroach walk: One, two, three, stamp! One, two, three, stamp! The other version was the "tenement tap," which stressed snappy toe work. A tiny black creature that seemed to have thousands of shiny, rippling legs would suddenly dash across the "white" enamel kitchen sink to some secret rendezvous. One of us was always on guard, folded newspaper in hand, waiting to deliver the coup de grace. "There it goes! Socko! That's eleven I got today." Mama always said they came from "next door." "Next door" said they came from us (never!), or from "upstairs" (maybe).

If the tenement mothers were prolific, the bedbugs were more so. Loath as Mama was to destroy God's little creatures, it was a question of their children against hers. Mama, who obviously knew very little about human birth control, tried every method from sterilization to mass insecticide to keep down the birth rate of the bedbugs, but to no avail. Neither fire nor red pepper nor kerosene nor poison gas could destroy the sex life of the bedbugs. On hot nights they drove us out onto the fire escapes and rooftops and had the beds all to themselves, there to proliferate to their heart's content.

The menace of the mice had to be handled through an intermediary. We entered into a gentleman's agreement with a cat selected at random from among the thousands of out-of-work cats who lived in the neighborhood. It was a commission deal. She (a fact we found out later) was to chase mice and we were to give her carte-blanche use of the garbage pail. We called the party of the second part Hamlin. She was sworn in by my father as she held one paw on the pail in the presence of the eight children as witnesses. The deal was a failure. Of all the cats in the world, we had to pick one who was a vegetarian. We caught her trading with the enemy, exchanging fish heads for cheese.

We just didn't get along with her. In the darkness Mama was always stepping on her paws. When she howled, Mama would say, "Who tells you to walk around barefoot?"

Hamlin's vegetarianism did not apply to her love life. She turned out to be quite a sex kitten. She was obviously out for more than the gentle stroke of a human hand (especially Papa's) across her fur. There were nightly serenades from the backyard fences—the call of the wild.

She often went AWOL, staying out all night. Mama was afraid we would learn "bad things" from her.

One morning there was a litter of kittens and more mouths for us to feed. We gave the kittens away but kept Hamlin, hoping that she would mend her ways. Soon there was a repeat performance. We felt that this was a breach of contract. We called a family council and decided to dissolve the partnership.

We did not throw her out. No, we tried to do right by her. We blindfolded her, put her in a shoebox, took the Third Avenue trolley, transferred at 125th Street, went west to Riverside Drive, and left the box in front of a home with a future. When we got home, about two hours later, there was Hamlin in the kitchen waiting for us. I'll never forget her look. For a dumb animal she made it pretty clear that we were not to pull this kind of trick again. We didn't. She stayed with us five years longer and had at least forty more kittens. When we moved she refused to leave. She stayed behind with her mice.

✣✣✣✣✣

The mothers of our tenement tried to bring some of the loveliness of nature into their homes.

Most of them had been raised in small country towns. They remembered the scents of hay, mint, and wild flowers as if, in some previous incarnation, they had lived in a time and place that was free of the summer stench of hot pavements and backed-up sewers. "I can't believe that there ever was such a time," Mama would say. "It's like a dream." Even the tenement bricks seemed to remember that they, too, had once belonged to the soil, and defiantly would sprout a few blades of grass through the cracks in the cement.

Every fire escape harbored a monster snake plant or rubber plant. Mama also had a century plant that had about two years to go. When it got sick she nursed it as though it were human. She poured mineral oil into the soil, and wiped each leaf with a damp cloth in an attempt to bring life back to the fading leaves.

Although Mama could remember, however dimly, a childhood surrounded by nature, her children would have no such memories. We were strictly city kids whose attempts at communicating with nature were pathetically ludicrous. Each spring we would write to our congressman for free seeds, which we planted in soil in cheesebox flowerpots. We called it soil but it was really a mixture of broken glass, gravel, decayed wood and mud that we found around construction projects. We poured gallons of water into the boxes—enough for an aquarium, but too much for flowers. The water ran down onto the pillows put out to air on the fire escapes below.

I came home from school one day with a narcissus bulb that my teacher had given me. I left it on the kitchen table and went out to play. On my return I discovered that a visiting uncle had grated it and was eating it with sardines. About an hour later he turned green.

Our schoolyard had a vegetable garden where we toiled like prisoners in the fields, learning to love nature. When the school announced it would lend tools for home gardens, we prepared to reclaim the desert in our back yard. We sectioned off the tomatoes, the stringbeans, corn, peas, cucumbers and radishes. By midsummer, where nothing had bloomed before, there stood giant patches of banana peels, chicken heads, corn husks, and mattress springs.

We made several tries at maintaining a goldfish bowl. Mama loved the restless little creatures. She insisted that they recognized her. When she came near the bowl the fish would swim up to the surface to be fed. Mama would let us feed them. "Remember, just two little pieces." For good measure we threw in a handful. By evening at least one little fish would be floating belly up on the water. "You killed him!" We couldn't understand how overeating could kill anything.

Some of the kids raised pigeons on their roofs. The women protested that the birds dirtied their windows. Nevertheless, whenever a pigeon landed on a windowsill, a red, work-worn hand would appear with a little heap of breadcrumbs for the emissary of Mother Nature.

※※※※※

I never heard Mama pray for anything but food and good health for herself and the family. She may have wanted roses, too, but she was afraid of offending God by asking for more of life than any of the other mothers on our block were getting.

I don't recall what the occasion was but somebody once sent us a bouquet of flowers. Mama gasped when we opened the long box. There, wrapped in green waxed paper, were one dozen roses nestled in ferns.

There were tears in her eyes as she placed the roses one at a time into a coupon-premium water pitcher with a slightly chipped handle. She raised each flower to her nostrils, inhaled the perfume deeply, and held her breath long enough to saturate her senses, so she would remember.

Then, as one under a spell, she shuffled slowly into her bedroom. When she came out her hair was combed and she had on a new dress. The tone of her voice was subdued. She even asked me to "please" run down to the grocery for a quarter of a pound of pot cheese "from today."

The thrill of live roses in the house was too much for one person to bear. Mama picked out three of the long-stemmed beauties, added a few ferns, and sent them to the next-door neighbor.

As each of the boys came home the same scene was enacted over and over again: "Hey, where did these come from? Ain't they gorgeous?"

"Don't touch," Mama said. "Just smell." And smell we did. All evening long we kept pushing our noses into the flowers until we smelled like roses and the roses smelled like us.

As the days passed the flowers began to fade, and Mama began to philosophize about how human beings were like flowers and how soon we all wither away and die.

Finally each kid pressed a rose between the pages of a book. Mama went back to chopping meat, and she stopped saying "please."

❦❦❦

Plants could not flourish in our flat, but books did. They grew and multiplied in the dark. They were displayed, dusted, protected, and referred to with reverence. I respected them long before I could read them. In this sense, again, I was a privileged child. I was heir to an ancient tradition of love of learning. Our household heroes were almost exclusively men of learning, spiritual leaders, poets, musicians, philosophers. We hung their pictures on our walls, along with our diplomas.

My parents told us how in the old country when a child began his religious education his first book was strewn with raisins and almonds as a symbol of the sweetness of knowledge. The first song I remember my mother singing to me was a sort of hymn in praise of education. It is perhaps the only folk song of its kind and it had to come from the "People of the Book." It was sung, naturally in Yiddish. I have put it down freely rendered as I remember it:

Around the Fireplace
There's a fire on the hearth
And the house is warm
And the little ones, all of them,
Learn their A, B, C.

Say it, little ones, say it, precious ones,
What you're learning here.
Say it once again, and even once again,
Say your A, B, C.

When you will older be
You will understand
How many tears have fallen on these pages,
How much heartbreak felt here, too.

Say it, little ones, say it, precious ones,
What you're learning here.
Say it once again, and even once again,
Say your A, B, C.

In my elementary-school-graduation autograph book Papa wrote in Hebrew the words "My son, make thy books thy companions. Let thy cases and shelves be thy pleasure grounds and gardens . . ."

I recently found the entire quotation. It was written by Judah Ibn Tibbon in twelfth-century Spain. It continues from where Papa left off with ". . . pluck their roses, take their spices and their myrrh. If thy soul be satiate and weary change from garden to garden, from furrow to furrow, from prospect to prospect, then will desire renew itself and thy soul be filled with delight."

Compulsory education was not regarded by my people as a legal imposition but as a golden opportunity—part of the dream that had brought millions of immigrants to America. The word "culture" brought tears even to Papa's eyes, but he could not make sense out of the stuff they were teaching us in school, like "The cow says, 'Moo, moo,' the pig says 'Oink,' the dog says, 'Bow wow.' "

"What's the matter with these animals?" Papa used to say. "Can't they talk English?"

My childish fingers riffled through the pages of books my older brothers were reading. I was awestricken by the big words, and I looked forward to the day when I might understand them. Children's books didn't come into my life until I had children of my own. I never read *Alice in Wonderland* until my children did. My "Wonderland" as a child was the mysterious books all about me as yet unread. I imagined what was in them. When I got to read them later in life I found them even more exciting than I had dreamed. I still open an unread book with delicious anticipation.

My older brothers used books as a ladder to elevate themselves to the point where they could see beyond our block. They stole a glimpse of the great, free world of ideas. Our bookshelves reflected the expanding intellectual horizons of the family. Papa's traditional prayer books were joined by Plato, Shakespeare, Voltaire, Tom Paine, Ingersoll, Tolstoy, Dostoievsky, Shaw, Dreiser, Whitman. . . . Papa must have suspected that some of the boys were going off in directions alien to his traditions, but he was tolerant.

We spent much of our time in the public library for two reasons: they had the books we could not afford to buy, and they had steam heat. I admired my brothers' library cards, which were heavily stamped with dates of withdrawals. This to my mind was status—a dog-eared, smudgy library card. I tried to match their record. I withdrew and returned books at the rate of two or three a day. I had to have a dirty library card.

And the humiliations I had suffered to get the card in the first place! I had to get references from my school principal and "two responsible citizens." I got the OK of the principal, but where was I to find a responsible citizen, one who, according to the librarian, had his name in the telephone book? I gave the candy-store phone number. That got me into trouble. I had to produce a birth certificate. Mine had been lost. They began to question my legitimacy.

When I took out my first book I caused quite a stir at the signing-out desk. At the secret request of my cousin Sophie, who was too embarrassed to do it for herself, I withdrew *What Every Girl Should Know*. The librarian put a question mark in red beside the name Samuel on my card.

✸✸✸✸✸

Culture was not optional. In a era when heads of families earned ten to twelve dollars a week there was hardly a family in our building that did not have a piano with a hand-knit shawl on it, and/or a violin. Practice was compulsory. "Practice! I'm spending Papa's bloodstained money on you!" All day long one could hear the voices of mothers screaming from windows: "Your music teacher is here!" If the reluctant virtuoso didn't show up, the kid brother had to take the lesson for him. Those kids who practiced willingly weren't safe on the street. There were trios and quartets waiting for them at the corner to teach them a lesson or two.

I was given violin lessons, and I knew where Mama got the money. She stole it from the "table money"! "Some day you'll appreciate." I appreciated Mama even more than I appreciated music, so I practiced. Since I played so badly that one melody was almost indistinguishable from another, she knew I was practicing only if she heard screeching sounds from the bedroom. I could bounce rhythmically on the mattress for a half hour and satisfy Mama's soul in the kitchen. I suffered for my art, too. Whenever Papa read in the paper that Jascha Heifetz got five thousand dollars for a concert, I got hit. "Practice!" Even the street musicians played better than I did. I used to give them a penny to move away from our window before Mama heard them and made me practice harder.

Along with most of the kids on the block I took my music lessons at the neighborhood "Y." At the end of each year the school gave a student recital at which we displayed the progress we had made. Most of us sounded no better than the previous year, but we were now making weird sounds from Book II rather than Book I.

We each brought home tickets for the concert. Mama didn't boast. She merely informed the neighbors that Sammy was going to "give a concert." There wasn't a single neighbor who thought that Sammy had any talent, but if he was going to "give a concert," maybe they had underestimated his ability.

These student-recital audiences were the best in the world. They loved every performer, that is, each family loved its own, but applauded sympathetically for all. The program was longer than a Wagnerian opera as originally scored, without intermission. It usually opened with "Flow Gently, Sweet Afton" performed on the violin by Paul Berkowitz, age nine, six months' instruction. The music flowed neither gently nor sweetly. He started without waiting for the piano introduction, covered the Afton in thirty seconds flat, and tore the house down when he bowed so low that his head touched the floor. He then exited the wrong way and bumped into a young cellist coming on stage. Grand ovation for both.

Then came more Berkowitzes, Murphys, Kowalskis, Angelinis, Thompsons, and Hoffritzs plowing through Polonaises, Valses, Etudes, Caprices for one hand, two hands, four hands and no hands. By this time the audience was cadenza-happy and tone-deaf.

As a reward for appearing in the concert, Mama told me I didn't have to practice for a whole week.

　　　　　❀❀❀❀❀

Not to be outdone by Pickle Week, Foot Care Week and Remember the Buffalo Week, some teachers' organizations have managed to promote a Teachers' Recognition Day. My parents did not need to be prodded by public-relations programs into an attitude of respect for teachers. I was raised to believe that teachers were infallible and superhuman. A teacher was not like a relative, a neighbor, or even a friend. When a teacher passed on the street the mothers stopped whatever they were doing and bowed their heads slightly in acknowledgment of her presence. The fathers, who rarely tipped their hats to anyone, did so in respectful silence to a teacher. She was above parents and just a little below God, and as such was held in the kind of awe that bordered on fear.

As a child I could never conceive of a teacher's being subject to the habits of ordinary people. We never saw her eat, or drink, or scratch, or blow her nose, or, perish the thought, go to the bathroom. Her conduct was as stainless as her stiffly starched blouse.

If there was an occasional parents' meeting in the evening Mama went, only to doze off during the principal's speech. She didn't have to listen. The principal was an educated person, and educated people could do no wrong.

"She knows what she's talking about." That was good enough for Mama.

The attitude of the teacher toward the parent was that of a professional toward an amateur. She would not think of asking the parent's advice any more than a doctor would ask his patient for a prescription. As far as the children were concerned, any sign of resistance to her hegemony over their minds and bodies was deemed a mutiny and dealt with accordingly.

A "B" in conduct was the equivalent of a scarlet letter. It meant I had offended God, man, and country. I was guilty of high treason. Mama would wring her hands in grief: "What have we come to? Look at me, bum, son of Cain, thug. Better to look at me than at a judge." Brother Joe joined in, "Whatsamatta? You a wise guy or something?" And brother Jack: "Making trouble for the teacher? Papa works all day in the shop so you can be a hoodlum or something?" And Mike: "Swear on your pinkie you'll never be bad again."

I was bad again. This time it was a matter of lateness. My teacher told me I would have to bring my mother. In those days "Bring your mother" were the most frightening words a teacher could say to a child.

I was trapped in a no-man's-land. Mama had said "If I have to go to school for you once more, don't come home from school" on the very same day that the teacher had said "Don't come back without your mother."

I appealed to the candy-store lady near the school. I explained that my mother was sick and couldn't come to school, and would she please act as my mother, for which my own mother would be eternally grateful. She came and listened to the list of charges against me read aloud by the teacher before the entire class. Mrs. Candy Store got carried away by her role and outdid my own mother. She turned to me in a rage:

"Is this true, all that the nice teacher is saying about you?"

Without looking up I answered, "Yes."

The stand-in then gave me a clout on the head like I had never gotten from my own mother.

I was late once more. At this point in my life, crime set in. I played hooky.

Experienced hooky players know what to do with their ill-gained time. I didn't. The hours weighed heavily on my hands. I realized that I had better get out of my own neighborhood. I walked for miles. It wasn't easy to find a neighborhood in which there were no mothers. I felt that all eyes were turned on me. "That's him!" I avoided all men in uniform: policemen, firemen, street cleaners, mailmen, Western Union messengers and milkmen.

I had no money and I was starved. Maybe I ought to run away from home, get a job in Bridgeport, become very successful and then send for the whole family, who would then forgive me in my mansion. How old did you have to be to join the Navy? I saw kids from other schools going home for lunch and then going back to school, some with a cooky in the hand. Lucky kids, they had mothers. I had disowned mine by playing hooky. Maybe Mama would die because of me. I timed my arrival home at exactly ten past three. My bread-and-butter was waiting for me as usual. Thank God, Mama was no truant.

The next morning I found out that crime doesn't pay.

My classmates greeted me with: "Where were you yesterday? We had a great time. The teacher was absent."

❀❀❀❀❀

The worst offense in class was to break the silence. Classrooms today are built with acoustical tile to soundproof the room. In those days they soundproofed us. There was comfort in knowing that no matter how many times you changed schools you could never fall very far behind. Punishments were uniform. You had a choice of standing in the corner facing the wall ("That will teach you a lesson"); writing "Columbus discovered America in 1492" five hundred times; staying after school and washing the blackboards (causing in the habitual mischief-maker a chronic case of dishpan hands); putting out your hand for a rap on the knuckles; being kept after school with your hands clasped on the desk till death (or teacher) do us part; or, in severe cases, being demoted an entire grade, where the work, at least, was familiar. There was no point in complaining to Mama about all this because she would only say, "That will teach you a lesson."

When the opportunity presented itself we were not long in rebelling against the strict discipline. Those were memorable times—especially the day the teacher said, "I have to go to the principal's office for a few moments. I trust that you will behave like ladies and gentlemen while I'm gone. Arthur will take charge until I return and will report any misbehavior."

Stoolpigeon Arthur, up there all alone silhouetted against the blackboard, made a beautiful target. A blackboard eraser made a perfect landing on his head and blinded him with a burst of powdered chalk. That was the signal. All inhibitions were wiped out in a sudden explosion of pent-up energy. From each according to his ability. The artists went to work drawing pictures of the teacher on all the blackboards. The air force sent out paper gliders in mass formation. The fire fighters splashed ink in all directions. One kid took the teacher's pitch pipe out of her desk and tore off a hot "Tiger Rag" while the boys paired off in couples to dance on the desks. The rhythm was supplied by the percussion division pulling on the window-shade cords. In the background could be heard the muffled cries of six girls who had been locked into the coat closet.

"Hey, Nelson! You be teacher." Nelson stuffed his shirt with paper to simulate the female form, made his rear end protrude abnormally, banged his ruler on the desk and shouted, "Clahss! We shahl hahve a two minute drrill! Breathe in! Breathe out! Knee bending! Ahll togethah. Down! Up! Down! Up!"

"Hey, fellers, she's coming," cried the lookout. It took about one millionth of a second for us to quiet down. You could hear the air humming. Gray-haired Arthur took over again and life went back to normal.

Our teacher's announcement that we were going to have an assembly was always greeted with joyous excitement. Give us anything but arithmetic.

We were paraded into the auditorium. A short and

plump teacher played a march on an immense piano that looked like a mahogany coffin with keys, while a tall and skinny teacher stood on the stage clapping her hands rhythmically, calling out, "Left, right, left, right." We would come down the center aisle, then separate—boys to the right, girls to the left— and wait at our seats while the color guard stumbled onto the stage. Then came "The Star-Spangled Banner," always followed by "Your singing today is very disappointing, children." We could not sit down until the tall teacher signaled with her long ruler. We came down with a crash and a burst of talking. "Class stand. That was very poorly done. Your sitting is very disappointing today. We shall practice sitting down until you can do it like ladies and gentleman. Ready!" Signal. "Sit! That boy in the back, see me after class. Stand! Sit! Stand! Sit! Stand! Stand! Sit!"

The principal, hoping to uplift us, would mumble a verse from the Bible, one that I have never been able to locate since—something about not smiting the Smithsonians lest thee thyself be smooten.

Without interruption she would then continue with "We have several important announcements to make. Classes 3B-2, 5B-1, 6B-3, 7B-4, 8B-1, 4B-5, 1A-6, 6A-1 and Ungraded 1 have all achieved one hundred per cent G.O. membership." (Applause.) "The Archery Club will practice in the lunchroom today during the lunch period."

The tall teacher took over again. "That will be all for today. Let us make our exit an improvement over our entrance. Class stand! Class sit! Try it again. Class stand! Girls will face right, boys will face left. Those near the windows will face right, those near the front will face back, those near the back will face front. Forward march!" We

all marched forward into each other. We were kept after
school for an hour to practice exiting like ladies and
gentlemen.

❦❦❦❦❦

Mama practiced medicine without a license but not
without a philosophy. The preservation of life was a religious commandment based upon the doctrine of the sanctity of the human body as the dwelling place of the spirit. If
the body housed the spirit, that house (like the apartment
we lived in) had to be kept in decent repair or the spirit
might become ill.

It was not just her reverence for life that impressed me.
I was touched by her reverence for *my* life. There was a
sweet sense of security in being worried about, hovered
over, and ministered to. In such a home no one could
ever die.

We were the recipients of Tender Loving Care long before the pediatricians and the psychologists and the pocket-
edition guides made T.L.C. a slogan. Our Mothercare
plan anticipated the Medicare plan by about fifty years.
Mothercare was a plan that used doctors only as a last
resort, after all the time-tested home remedies had failed
and there seemed to be very little hope. "Sammy was so
sick last night we almost called the doctor." I can still
hear Mama saying things like "He's a very good doctor;
may we never need him," or "The doctor got there too
late to save him. He recovered by himself."

Tenement mothers practiced folk medicine: an accumulation of collective experience, hearsay, improvisation and
common sense. Most of the mothers-in-residence majored

in physics. The outstanding miracle drug of that era was castor oil. If you as much as held it up in front of a sick child, he would immediately scream "I'm better, I'm better." Ex-Lax was much preferred and often taken surreptitiously. The taste of sweet chocolate in a kid's mouth was worth the penalty to be paid later.

The practices employed by Mothercare were standard: a mustard plaster substituted a new pain for the old one (when removed violently it would drag along enough skin to make your liver visible for a week). There were mysterious therapeutic virtues in foods like garlic and onions —which at best kept away people, sick or well. I remember kids wearing garlic necklaces or little sacks of camphor crystals around the neck to ward off disease. Classrooms smelled like cedar closets. To keep clear of germs the family used a sanitary cup from which we all drank.

Small red radishes, a natural source of central heating, helped keep you warm over a cold winter. (It was rumored among us that Thomas Edison got the idea for the incandescent lamp from his mother's radishes.)

Any remedy that made you perspire was good. You could not possibly get well until you perspired. "Try and perspire, Sammy." There was hardly a remedy that did *not* make you perspire: sugar and kerosene; a salty herring wrapped around your neck; a steaming teakettle next to your head that even made the wallpaper perspire; hot goose-fat rubdowns; salt water-and-vinegar gargles. In an emergency, cupping would be performed by a barber. It took about two weeks to recuperate from a recovery.

The stronger the medicine, the better it was for you. We were forced to swallow stuff that today would be marked "For External Use Only." If a little was good for you, more was better. If one neighbor took a medicine and recovered, everybody took it—and got sick.

When in doubt the neighbors were called in—socialized medicine. They were always available for house calls. It was quite a traumatic experience to be lying in bed surrounded by a tribe of lady medicine men in kitchen aprons calling out cures: "Make him vomit, suck a lemon, breathe into a paper bag, put his head between his knees, blow three times on his hand, hold him upside down, shave his hair off, pull out his tongue, pull down the shades, pull on his ear. . . ." If all else failed they suggested that the child's name be changed to throw the Angel of Death off his track.

One of the kids in the building had an excruciating stomachache. The neighbors brought in an old crone who "cured" people through exorcisms. She lit a candle, let the hot wax drip slowly into a bowl of cold water, studied the congealed formation with deadly earnestness, and announced as she pointed to the wax convolutions that "two intestines had gotten glued together" causing the boy's cramps. By this time the boy was so scared he threw up. This unglued his intestines and resulted in a miraculous cure.

When a fever was suspected, Mama put her lips to your forehead and estimated the temperature as either "nothing" or a "fire." If there was a thermometer anywhere in the building the neighbors did not hesitate to borrow it. Reading it was another matter. They held it in the sunlight, washed it in hot water to clarify the markings, or left it in the child so long that minor surgery had to be used to retrieve it.

They fought fire with fire. For a high temperature, hot

soup. Hot chicken soup was the panacea for all illnesses, the elixir of life, the first and last resort. The humble chicken was our family's bluebird of happiness.

One of the classic stories of that era—one which has survived to this day—was about the mother who bought two live chickens. When she got home she discovered that one of the chickens was sick. She did then what any woman with a mother's heart would do—she killed the healthy chicken, made chicken soup, and fed it to the sick chicken.

Mama believed that most illnesses came from "something you ate, no doubt." The cure was to get rid of the offensive something you ate, no doubt.

One of my brothers had a tendency to be irregular in his habits. When his stomach would swell up to the point where he looked like he was with child, Mama would ask the usual question: "How long already?" He couldn't give you an exact answer because his memory didn't function too well, either. "I think last Tuesday." This called for drastic action: operation bagpipe.

On the back of the bedroom door, suspended from a rusty nail, hung a chipped white enamel semicircular two-quart tank which had a spigot to which was attached a long reddish-brown rubber pipe that ended in a black bone. This contraption was known in our family as "the friendly enema."

Mama filled the tank with a concoction of hot water and soap, which was to serve as a gentle persuader.

In order for the operation to be successful the cooperation of all members of the family was essential. You see, the pipe was old and it had cracked sections that leaked, and other sections that had gotten stuck together and blocked the passage of water. At a signal from Mama the brothers took their appointed stations. Each man knew his job. Some closed the leaks, others opened the stuck parts. There was also a clamp that had to be released upon order of the man at the top of the totem pole, whose job included stirring the soapy water. "Ten, nine, eight, seven, six, five, four, three, two, one let 'er ride!"

Down below, at the end of the pipeline, facing us from the wrong direction, was our stagnant sibling.

By observing the water in the tank, the top man could judge how much was going in at the other end. At first, for some unexplained reason, the level of the water in the tank would rise and foam, then it would slowly recede. Two resident brothers down at the bottom would shout into the patient's ear: "Feel anything?"

"Nope."

"Put your head lower and inhale. Feel anything?"

"Nope."

"The tank is empty. Feel anything?"

"Nope."

We would finally withdraw all the equipment and stare at him in amazement as he got up and walked toward the kitchen.

"How do you feel?"

"I'm thirsty."

88888

We saw our dentist twice a year—once when he moved into the block and again six months later when he moved out. To keep our teeth white we chewed roof tar. This not only kept them shiny, but preserved them, especially those that remained in the tar.

One of the reasons we were afraid of the dentist was that everything difficult or painful in life was referred to as "like pulling teeth." I knew one thing for sure: if pulling teeth was anything like getting a penny from papa, I wasn't going to the dentist.

The dentist's office wasn't very inviting, either. Outside his office, suspended over our heads hung a big gold tooth with roots that reached halfway down to street level. My friend Harold said "D.D.S." meant "Dey died screaming."

If you got a toothache Mama used to take an old stocking, fill it with hot salt, and run it under your chin and over your head. The stocking always had holes and the salt trickled down your shirt and tickled your stomach. You left a trail of salt that led everywhere but to the dentist. "Why bother the dentist?" we said. "It's only a baby tooth; it'll fall out by itself." Many "babies" carried their cigarettes between the swollen cheek and the stocking. If you couldn't chew on one side you shifted to the other side, then to the molars, then to the front teeth. When there were no more sides left, you would still sooner go back to the bottle than to the dentist.

We ruined our teeth by using them as tools. Molars were excellent for cracking nuts; bicuspids were for straightening bent skate keys; canines for untying knots; and incisors for sharpening pencils.

Poor kids could get free dental care at the local clinic. The atmosphere was humiliating, especially when groups of dental students were addressed by professors who used to illustrate an astonishing variety of disorders in our wide-open mouths.

I found myself one day the central figure in an amphi-theater lecture on sympathetic pain. The professor's asser-tion that a bad tooth can cause pain elsewhere was never better demonstrated than when he touched my pulsating tooth and got himself a murderous kick in the stomach.

There came a time in Mama's life when she had to give up her last, loyal molar and get a complete set of false teeth. She had been living on stale white bread soaked in warm milk for years while she saved up the dentist's fee. But she had a wedding to go to and it had to be done.

First she had to have her last remaining teeth removed. She came home from the dentist with plaster still oozing from her mouth. "Laugh, children, laugh," she said, hardly moving her lips. "Some day you'll all be old and ugly like me. I once had a mouthful of teeth that shone in the dark, each one a pearl. The way I came into the world is the way I shall go—toothless."

The day of the new teeth finally arrived. Brother David gave the signal. "Here she comes, boys." What an ovation. "Hurray for Mama! Let's see, Ma. Open your mouth. Stick out your tongue."

She couldn't close her lips, she lisped, and for days she ate in pain; then she gave up both talking and eating. She addressed us in sign language. Finally the teeth were deposited in Papa's big shaving mug. Even there they stuck out over the lip.

Then began the round trips to the dentist. "Scrape here. File there. It's loose in the back. It's killing me in the front." Papa worked on the plates with his carpenter's file. We finally got the teeth to fit like a pair of old house slippers. Mama started talking freely again, so freely that the upper plate dropped right out of her mouth into the kitchen sink and cracked in half. Back to the warm milk. Mama was relieved.

❈❈❈❈

We tried to build up our muscles with calisthenics. Maybe we had to be poor, but we didn't have to be weak and poor. We figured poverty might run and hide if it saw our big biceps. Our walls were covered with pictures of strong men in tiger skins pointing their fingers at us: "Are you a He-Man?" "Do women respect you?" "I was too weak to walk, now I run a grocery store." When I was about ten years old I still had enough baby fat on me to be a campfire girl, but in the mirror, boy! what muscles! I used to stand in front of it and practice being tough: "Yeh, you! What you gonna do about it? Who are you looking at?" Bang! No Goliath was gonna push around this little David.

One morning we were awakened by a strange twanging sound in the bedroom. By the dawn's early light we found brother Mike exercising his muscles by stretching a long strip of rubber. He had come under the influence of one Bernarr MacFadden: "You too can have a beautiful body."

He used to do setting-up exercises in bed. Body flat, raise feet slowly up, count ten, slowly down, count ten. Papa walked in and found Mike flat on his back with his feet going in the air "riding a bicycle": "Whatsamatter? You got a bellyache or something?"

Mike took to eating carrots, celery, raw fruits, brown bread and nuts. He lectured the whole family on how we were getting old before our time. Papa said, "You work in my shop and I'll do exercise and we'll see who'll get old first."

Wearing eyeglasses, Mike told us, was old-fashioned. Eyes must be exercised like any other part of the body. He would sit there and roll his eyes as though he were having a fit.

He would put on a show for my friends, tearing phone books in half, lifting tables with his teeth, pencils with his toes, and weights by his hair. He must have overdone it, because he was the first to lose his beautiful black hair, two teeth remained in the tabletop, and his arches gave way under the weights. At seventeen he was beginning to look like MacFadden at seventy.

Brother Bill boasted guts of steel. He would walk up to Papa and say, "Hit me in the stomach, Pop, go ahead, hit me! It doesn't hurt, go ahead, hit me!"

"What did you do?"

"I didn't do nothing, just hit me!"

"Tell me the truth, did you do something?"

"I'll do something later. Hit me in the stomach!"

"I'll hit you when *I* like, not when *you* like."

Later on Papa did hit him, but not in the stomach. You couldn't tell Papa where or when to hit.

Papa sneered at our gymnastics. He used to watch us flexing muscles and say, "These you call muscles? Ha! Ha! When I was a young man I had muscles. Such muscles! I used to carry two four-hundred-pound sacks of flour, one under each arm before breakfast, in the summer heat through snow up to here! Muscles they've got!" I believed him. My father said it, so it had to be true.

At Coney Island Papa would look over the vast expanse of ocean and say, "This is an ocean? Ha! Ha! In the old country, right in back of our house we had a river four times as wide as this pond. I used to swim it back and forth from sunrise to sunset." I was sure Papa could still match his old record if he wanted to. It was just that it took him so long to get into the water (I caught him at it once) that there was no time left to swim the ocean four times before sunset.

※※※※

The love of food and the food of love were one in our home. Our sustenance, emotional as well as nutritional, came from Mama. Mama was food and food was Mama. We loved the hand that fed us. Her feeding us was an act of love, a bestowal of the purest affection. "Love and bread make the cheeks red." The very words spoken with the offering of bread were words of love: "Eat, my dear ones, eat." And her hand would touch her heart to indicate the source of the food—herself. Her self to our selves —the bond that stayed with us all our lives.

Mama believed in the survival of the fattest. Fat was considered a sign of health. Layers of protective fat constituted a reserve against the lean days that could be counted on. Any food that was not fattening was considered unfit for human consumption. A baby weighing eleven pounds at birth was a nice normal baby who could be relied upon to gain weight. The weighing of babies was a service provided by pushcart peddlers. The baby was deposited in the metal trough on the right side of the scale and weighed like vegetables: "He weighs twelve pounds and one small potato." Or, if he was weighed at the butcher's, his weight might be "fourteen pounds with the bones."

Ironically enough, Mama was the first one to be put on a diet. The calorie-cops caught up with her. She was an expert at fattening up, but this business of thinning down was a new idea. When the doctor told Mama "Whole wheat bread, one slice a day (dry), cooked or fresh vegetables, green only, no salt, and leave the grease out of your cooking," she stood there as though hearing a judge pronounce the death sentence.

And we kids, little sadists, loved to watch Mama munching lettuce and talking to herself: "These young doctors. What do they know? They only want to shorten my life. They should worry if I leave a houseful of orphans. No bread! Where will I get the strength to diet if I don't eat bread? Remember, children, be good to Papa. Let him eat whatever he wants. Don't do to him what the doctor is doing to me. Visit my grave at least once a year. I tried to be a good mother to you."

Food was also one of mama's weapons against the world of "junk" outside—homemade antidotes against the "poisons" of the environment. She ran a family Diner's Club where the menu and membership could be controlled by her. Eating "out" was discouraged because the food and the place were both beyond the limits of her jurisdiction, and therefore suspect—unless by eating out you meant eating a piece of bread and butter on the fire escape, or via airlift: "Ma, throw me down some bread and jelly" (later revived by the pediatricians as "demand feeding").

The fellow who wrote "Home, Sweet Home" lived on an unbalanced diet. Our home was not only sweet but sour, half-sour, sweet-and-sour, and salty. Each "grain" of salt was the size of a hailstone—the kind of salt used today to de-ice major highways. Along with tons of onions and cabbage, Mama must have chopped thirty-six chopping bowls into dust. The house was alive with the odors of burning carrots, frying onions, cooking cabbage, fermenting sauerkraut, dilling pickles and, from the sputtering coal stove, that aromatic mixture of bread baking on the inside and socks drying on the outside. Often Mama used to leave a pot of milk in the warm oven overnight. How secure a child felt to smell warm milk in his sleep; how close to life at its beginnings.

Intermingled with the odor of food I remember the odor of Mama's body—the odor of hard work, the unnatural odor of young flesh grown old before its time. Her clothes seemed to have taken on the odor of her body.

No merchant could fool Mama about the quality of food. She smelled the merchandise before she bought it. Corn should smell like butter, fish should smell like cucumber, and nothing should smell like fish. For the holidays Mama bought live carp; they swam in our bathtub for days. Mama had to do the killing herself. We could not bear to watch this operation. Even after the fish was cooking Mama used to look into the pot and say, "That's fresh fish! It's still jumping around."

Horseradish went with fish. Mama enjoyed preparing horseradish because it gave her an opportunity to go on a crying jag. This was one time she didn't have to hide her tears. It would all start when she began rubbing the large roots on the grater. When the tears started to flow all the bitter memories came back. She compared her life with the bitter root. Bitter, bitter, bitter—bitter before, bitter now, bitter tomorrow.

It took years to develop a taste for Mama's horseradish. The ability to "take it" was a sign of maturity. At first, merely sniffing the jar would have us in tears. With the years we took larger and larger doses until we had developed a sufficient number of antibodies in our system to be immune.

The selection of a chicken was a fine art. By a process of chiropractic pressure here and there (especially there), Mama could determine precisely when the poor fowl had gone to its eternal rest. She would raise the deceased's eyelids like a coroner and announce suspiciously, "I don't like the looks of this chicken." Then she would turn to the grand jury, the other women, and demand an indictment of the butcher.

Our great appreciation of Mama's cooking derived, at least partly, I am sure, from the fact that we had the rich appetites of the poor. We could make sparks fly off a knife and fork. "Ma, I'm hungry." "Good, good. It's a sign of good health if you're hungry." We could not conceive of bad food.

We did not need meat tenderizers; our hunger-honed teeth could tenderize marbles. We also knew what every poor kid knows, that if you eat slowly you eat less—especially if you are a member of a large family.

A good housekeeper like my mother never threw out

leftovers. It pained her to see any morsel of salvageable food go into the garbage. "If you start to eat something, you finish it. Don't you know that's the best part?" It was never the same part twice. Any part left over was "the best part." Mama denied herself the truly best parts of the chicken and would eat the unpopular parts ecstatically sucking the bones and insisting that "young people don't know what's good."

If we had a can of salmon for supper and there was a bone left over, Mama could salvage it by adding four old rolls, matzoh meal, four sprouting onions and two formerly green peppers. The result was "salmon croquettes." These croquettes behaved very much like the spansules in vogue today that operate on a delayed-reaction basis. When the rolls had been digested the matzohs took over, then the onions, then the peppers, then some ingredient which even Mama didn't remember.

With the very same items Mama could also create a delicious tossed salad. At some time during the night you were made painfully aware of why they called it a "tossed salad."

Like all kids we had a sweet tooth. We craved the commercial stuff displayed in bakery and candy-store windows. Mama baked a brown coffeecake with a high shellac finish. It was the sort of cake that was smuggled into prisons. It didn't have to contain a file. Any prisoner could have sawed the bars with the cake. Sometimes Mama succumbed to our vulgar taste and said, "Here's a penny; go and buy poison." There was a bakery in the neighborhood where we could buy unclaimed wedding cakes (what a story there must have been behind them) or yesterday's birthday cakes decorated with Happy Birthday to Bertram on top of six layers of pure plaster of paris and surmounted by bluebirds and a snowman wearing a black silk hat.

"Cheap Harry's" candy store next to our school offered bargains in prize bags which we picked out of a large barrel sight unseen. The little brown bags contained not only discolored chocolates and rock candy on a thread but a real prize—a clicker in the shape of a frog, a magnet-pencil sharpener combination, a magnifying glass, a compass, or a tiny white celluloid elephant which was supposed to bring us good luck.

When Aunt Bessie came to the house she would always bring a box of real, fresh candy. She was a nurse and got her patients' surplus gifts. We would gather round the box, drooling. We had to restrain ourselves from grabbing. "Take one each," Bessie would say. Then began the speculation. Which one was a caramel, which a cherry, which a cream? I always preferred those wrapped in silver paper, although they invariably turned out to be disappointments. Some gourmet amongst us would always take a peek at the lower layer in search of a rare taste sensation. To make the ecstasy linger I didn't chew but sucked the chocolate or let it melt slowly in my mouth. The multicolored candy box was saved for handkerchiefs, or stationery, or just for smelling.

Because of papa's observation that "it isn't so good with money as it is bad without it," we were all expected to bring money into the house. It was not so much a question of how much as how soon.

I shall never forget the change that took place in me

when I began to bring money home, money I had earned myself and turned over to Mama like Papa did. Today I am a man! I sat down in Papa's chair and proceeded to read a newspaper. I couldn't read very well, but I turned pages and yawned like a tired father. I even tried shaving but couldn't reach the mirror. I put some coffee into my milk and complained that it was cold. I finally passed the ultimate test. I put on my good shoes and Mama didn't say a word. I had become a provider.

I was about eight years old at the time, and the job was in a butcher store. When not in the giant icebox (a most refreshing experience) I delivered pre-plucked chickens to rich people's homes. The rich ordered their chickens by phone and I carried the orders (at three cents per order) over the border into the rich area, south of 96th Street. The poor, who lived north of 96th Street, picked and plucked their own chickens.

For the first time in my life I went to homes with electricity in them, maids, and doorbells that worked, but I never got to meet the rich people. They weren't home. I never met their children. They weren't home. Some of the homes weren't home—the windows were boarded or the shutters locked. The only one at home in those houses was a short man in a white jacket who opened the door about six inches, took the chickens, and closed the vault. I used to tell my mother about these things and she always sighed, "The rich know how to live. It's worth selling your last shirt to be a millionaire. But what's this about no children?" To Mama a woman without children was poor. She would throw a penny into the charity box on the wall for the sake of that poor woman. "But they have dogs, Mom," I would comfort her. "Rich dogs who watch the rich houses without people in them."

Mothers as an employer group had a pretty bad reputation among us workers. You dragged that market basket through the mobs, weaving your way between stands, pushcarts, and the other child slaves, never complaining, never once saying "Buy me." You delivered your mother and bundle, both doing well, back to the house, and stood there allowing the perspiration to run down your noble forehead, proudly waiting for your humility to be noticed. A piece of cake, never as payment but as a reward, was always forthcoming, but money? Not from a mother! Never. But why did she give some other kid a penny for carrying her bundles when you weren't around? Why? Why? "Because I couldn't give him less," Mama would say. "After all he's a human being." Or Mama would say, "I owe you a penny." Can you take your own mother to court? Don't think I didn't consider it at the time. Even worse was her "Remind me to give you a penny." Is it right for a child even to remind his mother that she owes him money? I thought I had her once. What a trick! I asked her for a penny out on the street. I figured she wouldn't turn me down in front of the neighbors. She did. I had forgotten that she carried her money in a handkerchief tied in a knot in her stocking. She turned crimson. "You want me to get undressed in the middle of the street?"

There were pennies to be earned by writing letters for neighbors who had not had the benefits of a formal education. I couldn't spell very well, but they couldn't spell at all. Their mispronunciation and my limited knowledge of the world beyond my block produced some interesting faraway places like New Georgie, Pencilwanyer, Mont Riall, Schenectakee, N.Y., My Army, Florida.

The letters were very personal, even intimate, but the women figured I wouldn't understand about such things as pregnancies, miscarriages, desertions, tuberculosis, or appeals for money. And if I did understand, I somehow also understood that I was sworn to silence by the fee of three cents paid me for my professional services as a scribe.

The corner candy store had a public phone that served the entire block. There was a tip to be made by calling people to the phone. The candy-store man (that's how we identified the shopkeepers: the candy-store man, the grocery-store man, the candy-store man's wife, the grocery-store man's daughter's husband's dog) would answer the phone, then turn to one of us kids: "Call Mrs. Gordon's daughter, the older one, not the younger one, third floor back."

Not all calls paid off. If the news was bad, the callee often fainted right on top of you and you were glad to get out from under alive without her two cents. Sometimes you got the wrong person out of the bathtub and got a wet wallop for a tip.

Our services as door-to-door salesmen were solicited by greeting-card companies. From all statistical surveys our area seemed to be ideal for the sale of get well cards, although we somehow seemed to get well without cards. We could have used other types of cards: Congratulations on Getting a Bed of Your Own, or Happy Second Anniversary to Your New Shoes.

We operated a coin exchange among ourselves—a sort

of Levenson Family, Ltd. "Don't tell Papa about the rip in my pants; I'll give you a penny." "Lemme blow your harmonica just once. I'll give you a penny." "Push me around the block in the baby carriage. I'll give you a penny." "I'll give you a haircut if you'll give me a penny." The penny circulated through the family, buying and selling services and favors, until brother David, even then more of a sporting man than the rest of us, walked out of the House of Levenson, spent the penny and bankrupted a thriving family business.

✿✿✿✿✿

Mama encouraged Papa to get out of the sweatshop and strike out for himself. So Papa struck out—over and over again. He tried his hand at business—the cleaning and pressing business—and never failed to fail. His career was the very opposite of the standard American success story. He used to start with money and end up broke.

We all helped Papa in his enterprises. I looked through his personal papers once, just once. In the middle drawer of his work table was a collection of documents attesting to his failures: expired insurance policies, canceled bankbooks, an IOU from a deceased partner, an unopened letter stamped "Immediate Answer Requested," a letter from an employer offering a wonderful job for a single man . . .

Papa kept a little black address book that listed his social and business contacts in alphabetical order. Such listings would wreck a computer today, but Papa could find whatever he was looking for in a flash. His system ran something like this:

A—Anybody not on other pajes.

B—Brother in Canada

C—Canada, brother in

D—Doctors, Dentists, Delandlord.

E—Lectric Co.

F—From customers money do.

He was too timid to be a businessman. He was afraid—afraid of partners, afraid of the rent, afraid of the customers, afraid to ask too much, and afraid to ask too little.

He disliked customers on two counts: (1) If they didn't bring their clothes in, he would say, "How do they expect me to make a living?" (2) If they did bring the work in, he would grumble, "Who's got the strength to work for them? They're too sick to press their own pants?" or "A woman should be ashamed that she can't make a pair of cuffs."

Some of the people on the block never knew there was a tailor shop near the corner because the awning in front of Papa's store read "Fresh Fish Sold Here." It had been there when he took over the store and he saw no reason for discarding a practically brand-new awning.

The only sure income from the store was a pass for two to the local movie, which Papa got for displaying a poster in the store window.

Other men were more enterprising and talented than Papa. They borrowed five dollars, bought textile remnants, sold them and made fifty cents profit. Then they went into stockings, no store, just a box under the arm and lots of friends and "connections." From stockings to underwear to shirts to ties and a pushcart. Then came a little stand outside a store piled with "general merchandise": razor blades, eyeglasses, and frying pans. Finally came the store with two rooms in the back for the wife and six kids. Someone always had to be watching the store while the family ate. There was a cowbell over the door that rang when a customer came in, followed a split second later by a voice from the back calling out, "Front!" Customers inquired not only about merchandise but about the delicious odor of the cooking coming from the back.

Our block must have had about twenty such "concerns," each run by a different clan as a family project. The father opened the store early in the morning, worked for a few hours, then went into the back for a bowl of soup and a nap while the mother took over. She, in turn, was relieved by the kids when they came home from school. Then the father took over again and worked late into the night. This schedule was maintained unbroken for years. A day off was usually explained by a crudely drawn sign on the door: "Deadth in Family."

❀❀❀❀❀

As long as Papa was at the head of the table we were made aware of the unity of body and soul. There were rituals surrounding the care and feeding of both. Papa would take a small piece of bread in his hand, say the blessing, sprinkle some salt on it, then chew it slowly, thoughtfully, gratefully. He would then turn to the family and give the signal for the beginning of the meal with the words "Eat and remember." Once again we had been reminded that man is not an unthinking animal, and home is not a stable—certainly not our home.

Friday night's dinner was a testimonial banquet to Papa. For that hour, at least, he was no longer the oppressed victim of the sweatshops, the harassed, frightened and unsuccessful breadwinner, but the master to whom all heads bowed and upon whom all honor was bestowed. He was our father, our teacher, our wise man, our elder statesman, our tribal leader.

I was aware even as a child that my parents through their traditions had the power to separate mundane time from sacred time, to declare one day out of seven above and beyond the slavish struggle for survival. What a sense of power for a man to be able to borrow a segment of time out of eternity, to ask it into his home for twenty-four hours, to feel himself transfigured by it from man into Man.

The transformation of time began when Mama would usher in the sabbath at twilight. As we stood there watching her bless the candles and murmuring prayers, we could feel the metamorphosis of a weekday into a holy day. The candles threw ghostly lights and shadows on the walls. The mystery and the magnitude of the experience affected our behavior. We stopped shouting and talked softly to each other without having to be told to do so.

For us kids the Sabbath also had a special secular virtue: we were not spanked on that day. Never on Shabbes. But after sunset you had better look out!

Mama's relationship with God was different from Papa's. He taught us to worship God formally, using prayers we had memorized. Mama's was an intimate, personal kinship.

God was her Father and our Grandfather. She appealed to God directly: "Dear God, how long will this strike go on? Have a little mercy. The children need shoes." Although she stood in awe of the holy word, she said her prayers as she felt them. When the fourth kid went down with the measles, she began to lose patience. "Enough already, dear God. How much do you think I can take?"

Mama transmitted her personal relationship with God to us. If I found a penny, it was because God wanted me to find it; if I lost a penny, I must have deserved it. I must help Mama with her bundles because God said, "Thou Shalt Honor Thy Father and Thy Mother." I mustn't fight with Henry because God said, "Love Thy Neighbor." I can't take Harold's bike because God said, "Thou Shalt Not Covet Thy Neighbor's Goods." "So why did Papa take away the dollar Aunt Bessie gave me for my birthday?" "Because Thou Shalt Honor Thy Father and Thy Mother," said Mama.

For the Passover our home had to be converted into a temple in which rites of all kinds would be conducted—prayers, feasts, songs, even games, all related to one of mankind's greatest epics—the exodus from Egypt.

Our home had to be cleansed of all traces of bread. Papa turned sleuth. We followed him through every corner of the house tracking down every last crumb. It was a sort of game we played with Papa, perhaps the only game we ever played together. We placed little pieces of bread on windowsills and in corners, then later pretended to "discover" them. The punishment was standard—death by fire. The bread-burning, too, was both a ritual and a game. Token pieces of bread were placed in a wooden spoon, wrapped in a cloth, and cremated in small bonfires on the street by kids who were paid a few cents for "buying" our bread and helping us purify our homes in honor of the arrival of the Passover.

As though keeping dairy dishes at a respectable distance from meat dishes were not enough of a job, Passover required the use of all "new" dishes, which were kept in old barrels in the cellar. Operation Dishes included pans, kettles, crocks, graters, sieves, buckets, knives, forks, spoons, ladles, chopping bowls, glasses, bottles, jars, mugs, jugs, platters, dippers, cake pans, coffeepots, teapots. The year-round dishes had to be taken to the cellar or to some other neutral place. After a dozen trips to the cellar, one of the brothers always asked, "Why can't we all just move to the cellar for the holidays?"

There was great excitement in removing the faded newspaper wrappings from the holiday dishes and recognizing the familiar designs. These were more than just dishes. They had a history, and they brought with them the promise of family living on a higher plane than we lived the rest of the year. Each played a part in the folklore of the Passover season. Our mouths watered with anticipation as we unwrapped each dish and foretasted the thrills, both gastronomical and emotional, which would be forthcoming when these inanimate utensils would come to life again as part of the symbolism of the Seder service.

About three days before the Passover there was a knock on the door: "Your order is here." The Israelites took less out of Egypt with them than Mama brought in for the holidays. We were prepared for forty years of desert living. For weeks we felt our way amongst crates of eggs, sacks of flour, farfel and matzohs—matzohs in closets, on mantel-pieces, under beds, under tables, under sinks, on the fire escape, on the piano: egg matzohs, plain matzohs, long matzohs, short matzohs, round matzohs, square matzohs.

My folks refused to accept the idea that good wine could be bought. Every year they brought home baskets of wine grapes which they squeezed through sieves, filtered through sacks and finally deposited in barrels next to my bed. During the night bubbles would burst and send heady little wine-breezes floating about the room. How could I ever explain to the teacher why I was late for school?

I don't remember just how long it took, but after a certain period Papa would taste the purple froth. He kept his judgment to himself until after Mama had tasted it. Then Papa would say it needed more sugar and Mama would say it was too sweet. The neighbors were called in. They, too, were divided into opposing groups of "too sweet" or "too sour." "Since when did you become a con-noisseur?" "This is vinegar, not wine." "You used the wrong grapes." "For whiskey it's too weak, and for wine it's too strong." "What is it?"

The folks thanked everybody and ignored the comments. But every night Papa secretly put in more sugar and Mama secretly put in more water. We had to secretly bring up more barrels from the cellar. The wine was still not sweet enough and too watery.

One Passover Papa gave up in disgust and bought wine. With a smirk he poured a glass of the commercial stuff, tasted it, then gave some to Mama to taste. "It needs more sugar," said Papa. . . .

The Seder was conducted by King Papa with the utmost

solemnity. We princelings sat around the table with Queen Mama, all of us looking cleaner and shinier and more vibrant than at any other time of the year. This was an important event, and by participation in it we became important people. We were retelling, as were our kinfolk all over the world, at this same moment, in the very same words, a chapter of man's search for freedom. The text was sacred and we repeated it with awe, reciting aloud our identification of the symbols of our history before us on the table: the bitter herbs to remind us of the bitterness of slavery; a little mound of chopped fruits and nuts signifying the mortar that went into the bricks with which our ancestors built the pyramids when they were slaves to the Pharaohs; the roasted egg recalling the sacrifices made in the temple; the roasted lamb bone symbolizing the paschal lamb the Israelites sacrificed on the evening before they left Egypt; beads of blood-red wine dropped into a bowl, the curses visited upon Pharaoh; and the matzohs, the unleavened bread our ancestors took with them into the desert.

In the wine-stained Haggadah before me I could see woodcuts of the crossing of the Red Sea, Pharaoh's terrified soldiers on horseback being swallowed up by the waves, Moses pleading for freedom, and Hebrews being whipped by their oppressors. Before I could read, I had already become familiar with biblical accounts of cataclysmic upheavals in nature, apocalyptic disasters, miraculous victories, dramatic chronicles like Joseph and his Brethren and Moses on Mount Sinai.

For me, the youngest child, the Seder service held moments of great fear. I had to ask the Four Questions.

The answers, which would be given in chorus by the rest of the family, explained the meaning of Passover. My brothers would become abnormally quiet to be sure to catch every crack in my voice. I could see the twinkle in their eyes as I rose to deliver the traditional paragraphs. "Wherefore is this night different from all other nights . . . ?" They were with me all the way, but they mischievously hoped for some small fluff as a subject of conversation for the rest of the year. While no applause was permissible I could tell whether I had done well and would be held over for another year by the enthusiasm with which the chorus responded, "Slaves were we unto Pharaoh in Egypt. . . ."

As the evening went on, the mood became lighter. Between dishes made with as much love as chicken fat, and much singing, aided and abetted by the third and fourth glasses of wine, and the children's game of treasure hunting for the hidden matzoh (afikomen) for a reward, this was indeed a night to remember. How good it was to be slaves no longer, to sing our songs surrounded by our brethren, to feel rich and magnanimous enough to announce, "Let all those who are hungry come and eat with us" (even though it meant cutting down my portion), to talk of days when "all men shall be free" and "live in peace," to welcome the prophet Elijah into our homes, to drink the cup of wine which we had set aside for him, and for me to really see the wine level go down in the cup as he drank. This night I belonged to history and history belonged to me.

Passover ended and we became ordinary mortals again. The dishes were repacked and returned to the cellar, the good suit was hung up in the closet, but the matzohs died a lingering death. There were still about a dozen boxes to be finished off. We took matzoh sandwiches to school, to the movies, to the park. We left a trail of matzoh confetti behind us for weeks.

The very same foods tasted differently after the holiday was over. The spell was broken. Life was different now. Papa was not going to be king again for quite a while; Mama was also dethroned; and while we kids were not slaves unto Pharaoh any more, the landlord was still around, and we were back in the tenement, just a little bit let down, not quite sure that this was real freedom.

We celebrated all religious holidays. Perhaps it is more accurate to say we observed them with the proper joy or the proper gloom. A secular party, however, a sort of holiday by choice rather than by tradition, was called for only by an event of maximum importance—a recovery from triple pneumonia; the arrival or departure of a close relative from a distant place; the acquisition of "second papers" of American citizenship.

Mama was so grateful to God for having spared her long enough to see "this blessed day," that she voluntarily took ten years off her life preparing a celebration worthy of God's grace.

Invitations were informal. "God willing, if we're all all right, and you're not doing anything, and your children will be well, and you're going for a walk anyhow and you happen to be in the neighborhood sometime on Sunday not too late because people have to go to work on Monday if there is work, God willing, drop in. If not this Sunday, next Sunday." R.S.V.P. meant only "Remember Sunday Very Possibly." And nobody came empty-handed—this one brought a cheesecake, that one a bottle of wine, and all brought their children.

What was a party without children? We were the major subject of discussion—This is Sammy! How I had learned to talk, to walk, to sing; how tall, fat, smart I had become in such a short time. There were the usual command performances. "Say hello to your uncle; stand up for your uncle; sit down for your uncle; play the violin for your uncle; kiss your uncle." And the nice uncle dug his bristly chin into your tender little cheek removing two layers of skin.

Mama urged all guests to get started on the principle business of the day. "Eat first; talk later." What seemed to be a lavish feast was only another example of Mama's ability to make a little look like a lot. Bread, of course, went before, during and after each mouthful of the more expensive stuff, as a sort of appetite depressant.

First came the appetizers (as though we needed an appetite stimulant). Chopped herring garnished with yolks of hard-boiled eggs, and/or pickled herring, and/or herring in oil, and/or in vinegar, and/or in brine smothered with onions, and/or cooked herring, and/or fried herring, and/or herring baked in a brown paper bag and/or just herring.

The main course embraced the three kingdoms—animal, vegetable and mineral—stuffed into each other. There was chicken stuffed with chopped meat, meat stuffed with chopped chicken, stuffed derma, stuffed necks. There was also fricassee of chicken livers, fricassee of hearts, fricassee of necks, fricassee of chicken feet, fricassee of fricassee. The soup, which in those days was eaten after the main course, was a semisolid liquid (intended to loosen the log jam and clear the way for more delicacies) containing egg croutons, kreplach, dough balls and assorted tropical greenery.

No fine line could be drawn between courses. Each ran into the next and all led inevitably to the compote of pears and prunes and whatever else was cheap that day.

Throughout the meal Mama flitted about the table modestly belittling her cooking. "The cake didn't turn out so good this time, right? Your fricassee is better, right? Too much salt, right? My next-door lady and her suggestions!"

If any guest stopped long enough to catch his breath, Mama was right there. "What's the matter? You don't like my meatballs?" The intimidated one loosened his belt and went back to work.

Finally the casualties would waddle into what we called the "front room" (brother Joe called it the recovery room). In a state of stupefaction the groaning uncles would sit on groaning chairs and send out medical bulletins: "Oh, my gallstones; oh, my heart, oh, my kidneys, oh, my liver" —the organ recital, the boys called it.

As each guest left he was given a package of food, a survival kit for the trip home, at most no more than a few blocks.

By 3 A.M. lights started to go on in kitchens all over the neighborhood. "The gas is burning," Papa used to say. You could hear the fizzing of the baking soda and the belches for blocks around.

You will probably wonder where Mama got the money for such family fiestas. She borrowed it—from the next-door lady who borrowed from the upstairs lady who borrowed from her next-door lady who borrowed from her upstairs lady whose husband was working. At times when nobody was working, Mama would simply start the fire in the stove, put up a pot of water to boil and quote the proverb of the month: "He who gave us teeth will give us bread."

There was hardly an area of our daily lives in which we did not feel the presence of our parents. In our world of play, however, they were excluded. Actually they excluded themselves, not out of a sense of hostility, but because it was understood that adults didn't play with children. Adults, in reality, did not play at all. Play was for children; work was for adults, work and trouble and worry and anger. As children grew older they were expected to play less. Full-time work meant the end of childhood. Many of the boys, Mike and Bill among them, who were beginning to go to work would bolt their dinners and rush out in the twilight to retrieve an hour of their vanishing youth in a hot punchball game.

We played on the streets in front of our houses. We didn't play "intelligent" games. Some of our scoring systems were insane to adults but perfectly clear to us.

Sane adults knew better than to try to understand our games.

We did not "participate" in "activities." We just had fun playing games we learned from each other such as:

1. *Weight Lifting:* The weight was an empty giant-size milk can which one swung to a position directly over the head, then raised up and down as the crowd groaned and counted 1, 2, 3 . . . 27, 28. Sometimes, as the muscle man got weaker, the can would suddenly come down and his head would go into the opening. It had to be pulled out by violent tugging. To keep the young athlete's spirits up during the rescue we banged on the can to assure him we were on the job.

2. *Johnny on a Pony:* One kid bent over and held his head against the fire hydrant while others took a flying leap onto his back. As many as thirty to thirty-five guys would pile up on each other in a variety of unaesthetic poses trying to keep from falling off by sticking their fingers into the nearest eye, ear, nose or throat. The human mountain had to hold on until all said in chorus: "Johnny on a pony, one, two, three," three times. Sometimes the game was called in the middle of the pile-up because the third player from the bottom had to go and buy a quarter of a pound of butter for his mother.

3. *Kick the Can:* You placed an opened food can, preferably with a sharp, ragged edge, on the curb and kicked it through the air while everybody ran bases. Sometimes the can hit one of the kids; then everybody ran home while the victim's mother ran bases in search of "who hit him."

4. *Horse Racing:* We didn't ride the horses, but they ran, anyhow, without benefit of jockey. One kid would

sneak up behind a horse and pull a hair out of his tail. The startled beast would leap in the air and start running down the street, wagon and all, while we placed our bets.

5. *Straw Hat Revue:* On September 15, the end of the straw-hat season, we would run a string across the sidewalk and knock off the straw "Kellys" of unsuspecting passers-by. One kid would grab the hat and punch his fist through the crown. The kid with the greatest number of victims was the winner, or the loser, depending upon whether he got caught or not.

6. *Target Practice:* We filled brown paper bags with water and dropped them from fire escapes on indicated targets, usually human. The explosion could be heard for blocks around, even above the screaming of the target.

7. *Making Electrical Magnets:* This was done by gently rubbing a dirty pocket comb across the rear end of a cat. The charged comb then picked up little scraps of paper. "Look, Ma, 'lectric."

8. *Tobogganing:* On snowy days you seated yourself on an ashcan cover and slid down the hill, spinning around like a top, your head clockwise and your bottom counterclockwise.

9. *High Jump:* Two boys held a clothesline taut. A third took a flying leap over the rope, usually landing in a cellar. If he didn't come out we figured he didn't want to play any more. "Next!"

10. *Follow Master:* One boy, usually the least sensible of the group, was master. The others had to follow him and imitate anything he did, no matter how outlandish. Whoever survived won.

11. *Train Ride:* One kid sat in a corrugated box while

another dragged him all over the sidewalk—no tickets, no sense, just fun.

12. *100-Yard Dash:* One kid opened the swinging door of the corner beer saloon and yelled, "Drunken bum, drunken bum," then raced around the block four feet ahead of the drunken bum.

13. *Waddling:* You placed your feet on the rim of an overturned milk-can cover and swayed back and forth, propelling the cover forward. We could go quite a distance this way—if the grocery man didn't cut down our speed by clouting us.

14. *Stove Spitting:* A purely winter sport and strictly for indoors. We would sit around the hot coal stove in the kitchen, pick a section of the stove top that glowed violet, then, one at a time, spit on it and watch the little bubbles go racing around trying to save themselves from extinction, getting smaller and smaller until they disappeared. No score. No winners. Lots of fun.

15. *Yumus and Imus:* "You mus' be the doctor and I mus' be the lady"—or any other variation of acting out adult roles.

We invented toys as well as games. With a little imagination ashcan covers were converted into Roman shields, oatmeal boxes into telephones, combs covered with tissue paper into kazoos, buttons and string into buzz saws, bottle tops into checkers, broomsticks into baseball bats, old mattresses into trampolines, umbrella ribs into bows and arrows, a chicken gullet into Robin Hood's horn, candlesticks into trumpets, orange crates into store counters, peanut shells into earrings, hat boxes into drums, clothespins into pistols, and lumps of sugar into dice.

The older kids taught the younger ones the arts and crafts of the street. By cutting out a section of a cheese box at one end and another section from the opposite end and inserting pieces of mirror at each opening you could make a periscope. If you looked into the lower cutout you could see who was following you in the mirror. You could also accomplish the same thing by turning around, but the captain of a submarine never did that, so why should we?

A hair from a horse's tail could be woven into a ring. It required about a dozen hairs to weave one. Since most horses had black tails, the appearance of a white horse could cause a run on the market. The white hair was woven into the pattern to give it a braided effect.

Peach pits found in the street were rubbed against the sidewalk to thin them down and then were shaped into rings. A bunch of peach pits could be worked into a necklace.

And there was poetry in our lives—rhymes for skipping rope, choosing up sides, bouncing balls, countdowns, magical incantations, nonsense verse, tongue twisters, for taunting and teasing, special phrases for good luck and birthdays and finding things. Many of the following verses can still be heard on the streets of New York:

> Ladybird, ladybird, fly away home,
> Your house is on fire, your children are gone,
> Except the little one under the stone,
> Ladybird, ladybird, fly away home.

> Teacher, teacher, I declare
> I see Mary's underwear.

Julius Caesar,
The Roman geezer,
Squashed his wife with a lemon squeezer.

Mother, Mother, I feel sick
Send for the doctor, quick, quick, quick.
Doctor, Doctor, shall I die?
Yes, my dear, and so shall I.
How many carriages shall I have?
One, two, three, four . . .

My mother and your mother
Live across the way.
Every night they have a fight
And here is what they say:
"Icka backa soda cracker
"Icka backa boo.
"Icka backa soda cracker
"Out goes you."

Good night, sleep tight,
Don't let the bedbugs bite.

Old lady, old lady, touch the ground;
Old lady, old lady, turn around;
Old lady, old lady, point your shoe;
Old lady, old lady, twenty-three skiddoo!

Yellow, yellow,
Kiss a fellow.

Blue, blue,
I love you.
Black, black,
Sit on a tack.
Green, green,
Eat ice cream.
Stick your nose
In kerosene.

I should worry, I should care,
I should marry a millionaire,
I should worry, I should cry,
I should marry another guy.

Ladies and gentlemen,
Take my advice,
Pull down your pants
And slide on the ice.

Finders keepers
Losers weepers.
Findems keepums,
Losems weepums.
Findsies keepsies,
Losies weepsies.

Teddy bear, teddy bear, turn around
Teddy bear, teddy bear, touch the ground;
Teddy bear, teddy bear, tie your shoe;
Teddy bear, teddy bear, now skiddoo!

Spell Tennessee:
One-sy, Two-sy
Three-sy, Four-sy
Five-sy, Six-sy
Seven-sy, Eight-sy
Nine-sy, Ten-a-sy!

Charlie Chaplin sat on a pin;
How many inches did it go in?
One, two, three . . .

Cinderella dressed in yeller
Went upstairs to kiss her feller
How many kisses did she get?
One, two, three . . .

I love coffee
I love tea;
I love the boys
And the boys love me.

Although we never felt "unwanted," there were times when we were public nuisances to the adults. There wasn't a kid on the block who wasn't wanted—by the janitors, street cleaners, pushcart peddlers. We were continually getting in the way of people. Some woman would be coming home from market, a loaded black shopping bag in each hand, when suddenly a baseball would land on her head. She would pass out cold on a heap of onions and tomatoes. While the women were pouring water in her face to revive her, we kids would frisk her for the ball.

We *had* to retrieve the ball. We knew what would happen if we didn't. A rolling ball came to no good. Some woman would grab it and dash off to the butcher, who would perform a public service—he would chop it in half with a cleaver. On school holidays, when the street was mobbed with kids, the butcher used to put up a sign: NO BASEBALLS CHOPPED AFTER 1 O'CLOCK.

When adult pressure became too great we would try to find a lot to play in. We had an instinctive aversion to fences. Our special preference was for any lot surrounded by a fence labeled DANGER. KEEP OUT. First our scouts would try to scale the barrier. One kid would climb up on another's shoulders and a third on top of him would call out his observations: "Garbage cans, lumber, no dog; would make a good ball field." Then plans were laid for getting in. First a hole was cut with a pocketknife, then a piece of lead pipe inserted and used as a crowbar from which two kids swung until one of the boards gave way. Then a skinny kid was selected to squeeze through first. He was followed by successively fatter kids until the hole was wide enough.

If the city took over one of those lots and made a playground of it, we lost interest.

Men raised on farms can reminisce about the old swimming hole. We city kids had to create our own. We used to open a fire hydrant. If we could keep it open long enough (first came rust, then water, then the police), there was a private swimming hole in every cellar on the block.

As soon as the water came surging out in full force we placed an empty barrel over the nozzle, directing a foaming geyser two stories high under which kids would run about hysterically, some in underpants, some fully clothed, performing mad dances, making wild faces, deliriously happy.

※※※※※

We kids organized ourselves into clubs. I belonged to an exclusive one. We had been excluded so often we decided to exclude back. We called ourselves the New York Athletic Club. A kid in the group suggested that since there already was an exclusive club by that name in New York, and since we might play them in punch ball some day, it might be advisable to change our name to the Mohicans. You might ask why we chose to be Mohicans. Well, our block already had several tribes of Iroquois, Seminoles, Aztecs, and Cherokees. We would be the first of the Mohicans.

Admission requirements for the club were very simple. Any kid who owned a bat and ball was unanimously elected president. If we (or he) lost the ball we could always impeach him.

For a meeting room we made a deal with the janitor. He told us that if we cleaned up the basement we could use it as a clubroom. We worked for three weeks carrying out junk and mopping the place. We even borrowed curtains from our mothers. When we had the place all spruced up, the janitor rented it out to a family of six.

We had a treasury, of course. We were supposed to save up for jackets, with MO on the front and HICAN on the back. Our dues were only three cents a week. We figured that by the time we were thirty-five years of age we'd each have a jacket. We passed a law to the effect that if any kid moved out of the building before he was thirty-five he forfeited his jacket.

In order to raise funds we ran a raffle. We spent our last penny and had little books printed: WIN A GRAND PRIZE . . . $2.50 GOLD PIECE. (Some kid said it wasn't enough of a prize, so we made it a $2.69 Gold Piece.) MONSTER BALL . . . THIS MEANS YOU. COME YOURSELF AND BRING YOUR FRIENDS. TED LEWIS MAY POSITIVELY BE THERE.

One of the kids said that to run a raffle we needed permission from the Government, so we sent a post card in pencil addressed "To whom it may concern, President of the United States." It came back marked "Not Found."

We stationed ourselves at street corners and solicited funds. Our own families wouldn't do business with us. They knew us too well, so we stopped strangers. "Take a raffle, mister?" They all took raffles. Their hearts were touched. One look at us told them we were refugees from some war-devastated area.

We collected $18, which was just enough to pay the printer.

We never held the raffle, the printer bought himself a jacket, and that was the last of the Mohicans.

❁❁❁❁❁

Every spring we organized our own May Party with the aid of one of the "big people." Titles could be bought. For a dime you could be king or queen. The less money you had, the lower your station. For a nickel you were just a fairy prince. My brother Albert had only three cents so they threw him on a stretcher which was carried by four "Red Cross" nurses. He wore a bandage soaked in ketchup over his forehead and acted out the part of a wounded soldier. Actually, only his feet showed above the stretcher, so nobody realized the "unknown soldier" was Albert. (Three cents wasted.)

The most colorful couple in the procession were the "Bride and Feller." She wore long white stockings held up precariously by rubber bands, a white dress, naturally, and a long veil carried at the other end by a flower girl who wore wax grapes from her mama's fruit bowl in her hair. The bride's black shoes, which had been painted with white polish, were now a tattletale gray.

The feller wore too-long black pants, a frock coat and sneakers. His high silk hat barely fitted over the yellowish bandage that went under his chin and over his head. The groom had the mumps, but "The show must go on!"

We paraded around the block twice and then wove our way in and out of the moving trucks to the nearest park. By this time kings and queens were bidding for Albert's stretcher.

When we reached the park the adults gave us hot lemonade, we danced around the maypole twice, and started back, looking not at all like children playing at "let's pretend" but like prematurely old little people who had long ago lost faith in fairy tales.

⸙⸙⸙

Every poor neighborhood had a movie house affectionately referred to as "The Dump." Admission for children was on a package-deal basis—two for a nickel before one o'clock. Dozens of two-cent kids would congregate outside the theater chanting the movie mating call: "I've got two. Who's got three?"

Some houses didn't admit children unless accompanied by an adult. Every time an adult came up to the cashier's window he was ambushed by a gang of kids pleading, "Take me in, mister." If he took us in, it served him right. No grownup in his right mind would go to the movies on a sunny afternoon to sit in the dark with only partially tamed animals.

We came prepared for a long siege, toting fat-stained paper bags containing salami sandwiches, hard-boiled eggs, or black bananas. In the absence of any of these I could lick a single salty pretzel through a double feature. It was one of my childhood's greatest delights.

The management couldn't have made much of a profit on us two-for-fivers. They could have retired, however, on the trade-in value of the stuff we left behind: hats, galoshes, sweaters, gloves, rubber heels, bean shooters, eyeglasses and underwear.

Once we kids settled down inside the movie house, there was no getting us out. We were there for the duration plus a voluntary hitch. In order to prevent us from staying on for four performances a man came around to collect our ticket stubs. We hid in dark corners or under seats until the collection was over, then resumed the vigil with undiminished enthusiasm.

We could never get close enough to the screen. Hundreds of us crowded into the first two rows, and watched the film with our heads cocked to one side. To this day I remember Tom Mix as a long, tilted cowboy. Even the crooked villain looked like he was on the straight and narrow. When the picture showed a cattle stampede we ducked under the seats to avoid being trampled to death. Everything was enormous. Even the rabbits looked dangerous.

Those who came late were herded in the back like cattle. When the picture ended there was a stampede down the aisle. Sometimes a stray broke loose and the ushers would round him up. The rest of them milled around in the back and went *Maaaa*. . . . There was always one empty seat, and always some kid who climbed over others to stake a claim on it, only to discover what others had discovered before him—that some kid had gotten sick there.

In those days cowboys were real tough hombres, rugged illiterates. Today's cowboys are capable not only of signing their names, but of embroidering them. The old-timers never ducked bullets; they just took 'em. The hero and the villain would meet in a disputed gold mine and fire two thousand shots at each other out of one pistol. Later, when the mining started, all they got for the first month was lead.

They were called silent pictures. Maybe the pictures were silent, but the audience certainly wasn't. When "talkies" came in, it was two years before we noticed the change.

We were a most responsive audience. You could tell what was happening on the screen with your eyes closed. When the hero appeared, everybody cheered. If it was the villain, everybody booed. When the hero kissed the girl, four hundred kids kissed their elbows. If you heard catcalls, it meant somebody had let in a cat. If you heard sobbing, it meant the hero's best friend was dead. And if the audience to the last kid stood up and threatened violence, it meant the film had broken. Numbers would fly across the screen: 4, 9, 2, followed by a sign, BABY CRYING OUTSIDE.

The piano player in the pit tremoloed away as two cars chased each other on a high cliff. We screamed warnings, we screamed approval, we screamed at each other. Fights broke out. We stamped, we whistled, we wept when the faithful dog whined over his master's wounded body. During the love scene we went to the bathroom.

The Tarzan serials went on for years, and we lived in suspense from week to week.

"Please, Pa. I gotta go. It's a Tarzan."

"You'll go next week."

"I left him hanging over a canyon. Let me go!"

"He's been hanging since last Sunday, so he'll hang till next Sunday."

We talked all week about the possible ways in which our hero might be saved. We knew he would be, but how? Maybe he wouldn't be? We awoke screaming in the night "The train is coming!" Papa called us lunatics, but after we got home from the movies even he wanted to know how the guy escaped. Every week another miracle. The train was derailed, killing everybody, but our hero survived. They pushed him out of an airplane, twenty thousand feet up, but fortunately he landed on his feet. The elephant siphoned off the water from the swamp and our hero walked away dry as a bone.

Somehow, in spite of the limited funds at our disposal, we managed to cover every opening. We couldn't all go, so my brothers held a council and sent one of the clan, selected not by chance but for his good memory. He was given a briefing and orders to concentrate and remember so that he could repeat the entire story for the rest of us. Believe me, the kid who went to the show never enjoyed it. He sat there like a court stenographer, aware of the fact that if he forgot anything he would be held to account.

At 5 P.M. the council reconvened:

"O.K. Let's go. What was the name of the picture?"

" 'Trouble at Sundown.' "

"Good. Who was in it?"

"William Farnum."

"Great. So what happened?"

"So the bad guy he rustles, so the good guy he rustles back at him; so the good girl thinks that he is really a bad rustler, but he is really a good rustler; so the good horse goes to the good girl with a note from the good rustler, but the bad rustlers rustle the good horse and tie him up; so the good dog comes and unties the knots and tries to take the note to the good girl; so the bad rustlers rustle the dog; so the good girl goes out to see what's all the rustlin' about so they rustle her too . . ."

"So where was the posse?"

"There wasn't no posse."

"Whatsamatter? You holding out on us? Where was the posse??"

"I swear! There was no posse! Only good Indians, no posse!"

"That's what you get for sending that shnook. No posse! You'll never go for us again!"

❀❀❀❀❀

Since there was no sense in waiting for Mama to take us to Coney Island, we usually went by ourselves, or, as

Mama said, "Alone." Anywhere you went without your mother was known as going "alone," even if there were thirty of you.

We usually wore our bathing suits under our pants. If we had a nickel we went to the Municípal Baths, where the ticket-taker unintentionally humiliated us by requesting that we check our "valuables." I had no idea what a "valuable" was, except for the valuable nickel I had just handed over.

Going into the ocean was an ordeal. Its vastness and un-familiar beauty were beyond our physical and emotional experience. We stood for some time up to our knees in the surf trying to determine the nature and intention of its undulations before we risked a total commitment. Each wave seduced us just a little bit more, enticing us inch by inch, lapping our knees, then our thighs, then our stom-achs. By the time the billowy green-eyed Lorelei had her tingling fingers about our necks we were blue with cold and fear. We fled back to dry land and devoured our sandwiches like men rescued from a disaster at sea. I have never enjoyed food nohow, nowhere, no more, since. For me sanded pickle still remains seafood at its best, next only to cream cheese and sand-wich.

The one day at the beach when we had an extra nickel we gave it to brother Albert and told him to get a bottle of soda pop, "and remember, eight straws." Albert was gone so long we thought he was lost, so we ate his sand-wich. If you wanted to eat you had to "stick with your sandwich." Albert finally showed up with the nickel still in his hand. "Costs six cents," he said apologetically. The deal was off. We quenched our thirst on the saliva that had accumulated in anticipation of a strawful of cold soda.

For rich people on private beaches the sun shone on, a big, beaming father watching his children at play. On the public beach it rained. By two in the afternoon the dark clouds and the thunder were there, on schedule. We pulled our clothes over our wet suits and ran for shelter under the boardwalk, where we waited for fate and the weather to show a little mercy. Neither obliged. No sooner were we back in our subway clothes than the sun would reappear.

We proceeded to the customary march on the boardwalk —sand in our shoes, the sea still dripping in our pants, hunger loyally marching along with us. As Papa used to say, "Hunger will stick to you, even after all your friends have deserted you." The enticing odors of taffy, potato chips and frankfurters tantalized our senses. Once, in a fit of food frenzy, we spent our carfare on a frankfurter—the great American equalizer-tranquilizer.

The Penny Arcade was our Monte Carlo. If we had a few pennies we could pool them and invest in an ecstatic half hour, sharing the thrills among us. We had our collective future predicted by a wax gypsy in a glass case who looked like Mama. We watched spellbound as the gypsy's wrinkled hand tremblingly touched a jack of spades and a printed card popped out of a slit. "You will travel far. Have the courage of your convictions and you will succeed in the enterprises you are about to undertake. Be careful of Tuesdays." We weren't doing too well on any of the other days.

For the hundredth part of a dollar you could test your lungs on a Strength Machine. You blew into a mouthpiece and little signs lit up grading your virility: Boy, Henpecked Husband, Ladies' Man, Lover . . . Just as my eyes were becoming permanently crossed, the machine rated me as the He-Man Type.

There was a miniature crane in a glass enclosure which was supposed to pick up jellybeans, binoculars, cameras, gold rings and wristwatches. You operated the machine by a crank. The trick was to maneuver the crane so that its teeth clamped onto a valuable object, raised it, and sent it down a chute to you. I once won two jellybeans, one with tooth marks in it. On another occasion the world was almost mine. The crane hovered over, latched onto and finally raised a gold wristwatch, which it swung tremulously through the air and was about to drop into the chute when the machine's guts quivered and a sign lit up reading OUT OF ORDER.

There were games we could play without any money such as studying ourselves in the crooked mirrors and screaming as we saw a fat brother become suddenly converted into an undernourished nine-foot giraffe.

One kid would weigh himself for a penny and "sneak" us all onto the scale. We weren't sure that we each weighed forty-seven pounds, but that was good enough for free.

On the way home one Sunday, Albert found himself stranded on the subway platform. The door had closed, leaving us in the train and him out. He began to cry. Passers-by were sorry for him, patted him, and gave him pennies. The harder he cried the more pennies he got. He shied away from people who offered to take him home. He played the role of the lost child brilliantly. The following Sunday he was back at the same platform. When we got wise to his racket he paid us off to keep away from his territory. "Scram, this is *my* station!"

I still love going to Coney Island with my children. I

gorge myself on frankfurters, hamburgers and the other indelicacies I couldn't afford when I was a boy. I come home sick but happy. My children don't understand it; my brothers do.

❁❁❁❁❁

My parents never went out in the sense of "out" to a place away from home for fun and frolic. They rarely went to the theater. When they did go, it was not for themselves (which would have amounted to self-indulgence) but because Papa's lodge had taken tickets for a benefit—someone else's benefit—war orphans, a hospital, or a home for the aged.

The tickets were left in the cut-glass bowl on top of the icebox. Invariably, a half hour before departure the alarm went off: "The tickets are gone!" They were usually found under the icebox glued to the damp boards, smudged and discolored. Mama ran a hot pressing iron over them and they were almost as good as new.

Papa was usually ready by 6 P.M. At 8:30 P.M. Mama was still getting dressed. Papa sat in the dining room and fumed. Mama said Papa was a nervous man and that she was made of iron to be able to put up with him all these years. Papa, in turn, said it was no use trying to make a "lady" of Mama. "Other couples go out all the time." Because of her he was "buried in the house."

Naturally they could not afford good seats. Rich people walked in through the front of the theater. My folks were required to take a side door marked "Exit." At each landing a different usher tore another piece off the ticket and pointed upward. When they reached the second balcony the usher still pointed upward. Mama had to rest at each landing. By the time she reached her seat the play was well into the first act.

Papa preferred light comedy, dancing, music and a happy ending. His reaction to serious drama was, "I got my own troubles." Mama went to the theater to cry.

The folks sometimes took me along on what was called a half ticket. I sat half on Mama's knee and half on Papa's.

The Yiddish theater was truly a folk theater. The mythology of the old world and the new was familiar, the types recognizable, the problems standard. As in the Greek theater, the audience knew the subject matter and could foretell the ending of each play, but they reacted intensely and audibly to every development on stage: "Good for her! No! Yeh! Oh my! Look out! Again? Serves him right!"

Most of the plays told the story of immigrant parents and their problems with their "Yankee" children, who were usually depicted as first-generation selfish ingrates.

In Act I, the old father is cheated of his money by his children and committed to a home for the insane. The son is a bum: "Shoot me a buck, Pop, I got a date with the boys on the corner." The daughter is having a clandestine affair with a gambler who comes out from behind the china closet to demand a payoff. It is implied that she is with child by him.

In Act II, they get rich. This fact is attested to by having the curtain rise on a "fancy" living room containing an upholstered couch, a floor lamp, and a grand piano. The telephone rings, a butler comes on and answers the phone:

"Madame is not in." This in itself was enough to make the audience hate her. Any woman "not in" was a tramp. The "Mahster" wears dinner pants and a cutaway, the daughter struts about in a silk dressing gown, and a little boy in a Lord Fauntleroy outfit is playing on the floor. Everybody in the audience is whispering "That's her present from him."

But the play has a "happy ending." They lose their money and move back to the slums. No more telephone, nine people in two rooms, but their souls have been saved. The moral of the play was unmistakable: "Money is not for poor people."

When Papa went "out" alone it was usually to a meeting of his lodge. It was one of those small fraternal orders which hardly needed a constitution since the name of the organization set forth its entire program—The First Independent Mutual Sick Benefit and Burial Society. Papa's lapel proudly displayed the button of the organization—two hands clasped in a gesture of brotherly love and friendship over a tombstone bearing the initials F.I.M.S.-B.A.B.S. in practically gold letters.

Men whose talents were lost in the sweatshops here became officers, executives and committeemen, every man an orator. Dare to deny anyone "a word" and indignation ran high; "What kind of a dictatorship are you running here?"

"You are out of order."

"The truth is never out of order."

"Please address the chair."

"I'm not talking to chairs. I'm talking to my misled brothers in the lodge. Throw out this rotten clique!"

Every year they held a charity banquet. First the organization had a special meeting at which the membership voluntarily voted to force itself to attend, e.g., each member was taxed one ticket. This insured Standing Room Only. A few days later a formal invitation (usually a post card) came in the mail. "The F.I.M.S.B.A.B.S. Cordially Invites You to Attend the Silver Anniversary Jubilee Super Gala Charity Installation Banquet and Dance." The dinner was announced for 6 P.M.; and they didn't mean 8 P.M.; they meant 10 P.M. The band was hired for 11 P.M.—"Who's gonna dance?"

Seating the members required the wisdom and diplomacy of a King Solomon. There were ancient tribal rivalries. The president doesn't talk to the vice-president because of something he said that "he should have had more sense than to say without first hearing the other side of the story." The vice-president can sit next to a neutral like Mr. D., but Mr. D. can't sit on the dais because he is not a charter member. What's right is right. The vice-president should be at least at table 1, but table 1 is near a window. The vice-president has to avoid drafts because he sweats a lot when he eats. So they put him at table 2, where he goes into his soliloquy: "I'm not the kind of person who looks for honors. Maybe others, not me; I don't care. In this organization we are all equals. But to seat me next to an idiot like brother M————"

The climax of the evening was the installation of the

new president. The toastmaster rapped his gavel on the water pitcher:

"Fellow brothers and fellow sisters. I'm not a man for speech-making. At my house it's my wife who makes the speeches. (Everyone laughs but his wife.) Tonight I have the pleasure to install a man who, who, who . . . any time, anywhere was always ready. Wake him in the middle of the night he was ready. And now we are ready for him. Mr. ———, are you ready?"

(In a voice choked by phlegm and stage fright) "Ready."

"Are you willing?"

"Willing."

"Are you strong?"

"Strong."

"Then raise your right hand and repeat after me: " 'In the name of the F.I.M.S.B.A.B.S. . . .' "

" 'In the name of the F.I.M.S.B.A.B.S. . . .' "

" 'I will uphold . . .' "

" 'Uphold . . .' "

" 'Defend . . .' "

" 'Defend . . .' "

" 'Protect . . .' "

" 'Protect . . .' "

" 'The constitution of the F.I.M.S.B.A.B.S.' "

" 'The constitution of the F.I.M.B.S.A.F.M.' "

" 'I will care for . . .' "

" 'Careful . . .' "

" 'The hungry of the whole world.' " (This poor soul can barely support his family.) " 'I will fight to the last ounce of my strength.' " (He's getting weaker.) " 'I will protect my country single-handed if necessary.' "

('Maybe I should have been vice-president.') "I'm repeat-ing!"

"I give you the gavel of this organization; use it wisely."

The new president reaches for the gavel and doesn't make it. The symbol of his authority falls square into the anniversary cake with a sickening *shlosh*. Applause. "Speech! Speech!"

(Completely delirious by now) "I will give my blood and strength to the F.B.I.S.M.F. and will feed the hungry of the world, I will uphold, protect, gavel and defend. I will fight . . . fight . . . fight . . ." He collapses amidst acclaim.

If the folks had to leave us "alone" for an evening, there was no baby-sitter problem. We sat for each other. It would have made no sense to bring in a ninth child to sit with the other eight. Mama felt that if Heaven saw fit to give her eight kids to look after, she could impose upon Heaven to baby-sit for her once in a while.

When the folks left they usually appointed one kid deputy sheriff with power of attorney. They swore him in and recited the rules for all of us to hear: "The jelly is in the icebox, the milk is on the windowsill, don't play with knives, don't play with matches, don't spit out of the window, don't open the icebox."

The concluding bit of advice always was "If anybody knocks on the door say nobody's home!" We used to drive people out of their minds. Somebody would knock on the door and eight kids would yell, "Nobody's home."

What did we do all night, left to our own limited resources? We played games like Who can lean out of the window farthest? Or we threw a party, a spontaneous blowout—we lit the burner on the summer portable gas stove. Everybody yelled "Happy Birthday" and blew out the gas. Once we nearly blew out the kitchen.

We invented exotic menus: fried pickle delight, mashed-potato sandwiches, filet of tomato herring on lox. For dessert we made fudge—our way (you were permitted to eat the recipe while making it)—lots of peanuts, with or without their shells, chopped into a bowl, as much white sugar as Mama had in the house, and cocoa for color. If it got too dark, more sugar. If it got too light, more cocoa. (This did not insure quality, but it sure did guarantee quantity.) Finally, milk was added and the entire mess stirred all over the kitchen table, chairs, walls and floor. The surplus was scraped off the hands with a carving knife which you then gave a favorite brother to lick.

By 10 P.M. we were overfed, overexhausted, and under-oxygenated. We didn't fall asleep, but, like figures in a fairy tale under a spell, each came to a halt in a state of suspended animation, eyes open, hands inert.

By midnight the folks came home. As usual, Papa thought Mama had the key, and as usual Mama thought Papa had the key. One night, they couldn't get in. At first Papa knocked gently on the door so as not to wake the neighbors. That didn't get any results, so he started calling us by name: "Sammy, Albert, Mike, Bill." Then came more familiar names, "Dopes, stupid heads, open the door!" Papa blamed the children on Mama. *Her* children.

Mama smelled gas. "Gas!" The alarm spread through the building. People ran out with handkerchiefs over their faces. Papa looked into the keyhole. We might still be alive. "You wanna sleep, sleep, but lights cost money, shut off some of the lights!" Mama's hysterical pounding on the door roused Albert. "Nobody's home." Then he came to. He opened the door, and Papa gave him a hello on the head that put him back to sleep.

※※※※※

When our parents went to visit relatives they usually took only the youngest, Albert and myself. Riding on the open platform of the elevated train provided some unforgettable sight-seeing along the Third Avenue line. At some points you could reach out and touch the buildings. I wondered how people could live so close to the screeching wheels of the train. We could see into their homes. It was like a living moving picture. As we passed each window we caught a glimpse of the private lives of this great mass of poor people. Here a girl undressing (we hoped the train might stop but it never did); there a smoked-filled room, with men in undershirts playing cards; dark people in dark beds in dark bedrooms; a dog barking furiously at us as we passed; clean, ragged laundry drying on dirty fire escapes; children hanging precariously out of windows. Sometimes the train stopped between stations and we stared at these people and they at us. They were like animals in a zoo, quiet, accustomed to their captivity. I would feel relieved when the train began to vibrate and we moved on and away.

I shall never forget the faces in those windows. They disturbed me even as a child. We were poor, too, but these were the passive poor, the vanquished, the defeated, resigned to poverty. For them tomorrow would be as poor as today. In my home tomorrow was going to be better. We were sold on the idea that we could somehow erase the handwriting on the wall and scribble a few thoughts of our own on the subject of our destiny.

⌗⌗⌗⌗⌗

Emotional maturity comes early to those who are raised in large groups. Constant exposure to large numbers of people sharpens one's understanding of the nature of man.

It would be difficult for an outsider to conceive of the intricacy of our involvement in each other's lives. It was impossible to live alone or to die alone. Life was celebrated by all and death bemoaned by all. "Who died? How old was she? Did she leave any children? How old? Who's going to take care of them?" We operated on the assumption that if you didn't go to people's weddings they wouldn't come to yours, and if you didn't go to people's funerals they wouldn't come to yours. If a woman was sick, the neighbors fed her children; if the truant officer came snooping around, the kids tipped off the fugitive from justice; if the mailman brought a postcard everybody read it, and if it was a letter we took the stamps.

Our block, like the world, was a stage on which we saw enacted all the tragedy a human being can bear as well as all the comedy one needed in order to survive all the tragedy. Years later, when I began taking lit. courses in college, the subject matter struck me as familiar. Between the neighbors on the block and my relatives I had become acquainted with every plot, every motivation, every conflict and every resolution. I had already met the prototype of every saint and every villain.

There was the time Helen, next door, fell down the coal chute and talked wildly for days very much like Alice in Wonderland. My parents' stories of the Russian Revolution matched the passion and wild vengeance of *A Tale of Two Cities*. The accounts by various uncles of their flight from oppression across frozen rivers matched some of the scenes in *Uncle Tom's Cabin*. We saw ill-fated romances with as much beauty and passion as *Romeo and Juliet,* and ambition as ruthless as Lady Macbeth's. In our building there were a couple of Shrews who were being Tamed, and one jealous Othello who choked his wife because of an iceman.

The neighbors provided for each other whatever social services circumstances required—the temporary adoption of children whose mothers were incapacitated, marriage counseling ("Leave him? Never! Make him suffer like he made you suffer."); group therapy ("What can we do to help each other?").

The women "minded" everything and anything, without charge: "Please mind my fish, my soup, my husband, my purse." For me, there was an emotional affinity between being minded and being loved. While I did not like to be watched, I felt that I was being protected one hundred times over by one hundred watchful mothers.

There was also a Borrowing and Exchange Service that permitted the borrowing of even the most personal things:

hot-water bags, bath sponges, eyeglasses, even children. "May I borrow your Georgie to carry my bundles upstairs?" "May I borrow your window? I want to call my Harold for supper."

There were people who made a profit on borrowing by sending the father to borrow a "handful" of sugar and returning it by hand via little Annie, two years old.

There was poor Mrs. Burns, a widow, whose daughter was "going steady." When the time came for Mrs. Burns to invite the young man's family over for dinner she came to Mama and asked, "May I borrow your husband for the evening? I need a father to sit at the head of the table."

Our parents, and we through them, felt the security of this kind of "togetherness" born of necessity. Mama would say to one of the neighbors, "Come and sit with us." No Mah-Jongg, no bridge, no hi-fi, no cocktails, no television, no charades—just sitting. The kitchen stove made gentle static while the neighbors sat and talked. The men folk talked separately about their world: jobs, bosses, foremen, slack—"All year long you wait for the season, comes the season, no season."

The women peeled apples in long unbroken curls, munched them with their remaining teeth and discussed labor problems—three days with the first one, four hours with the second, true and false pregnancies, all the while pointing accusingly with their thumbs at "them," the men, the source of their problems. When the conversation got too intimate, Mama would nod in our direction, mumble "the children," and spoil everything just as it was getting interesting.

Each neighbor had some identifying characteristic. We

knew some by the odor of the cooking that seeped into the hallways. 'Uh-huh!" Mama would say. "Mrs. S. is frying onions." She became "Mrs. Onions." Mrs. Y. was always ironing and the odor of burnt cloth permeated your nostrils as you passed her door.

We knew the neighbors also by the way they knocked on our door. There were fist bangers, knuckle knockers, palm slappers, fingernail tappers. If there was no knock at all we knew it was the landlord. He never knocked.

Other neighbors were identified by sounds. Mrs. G. was always chopping food. Mrs. B. could be heard at almost any time at her washboard—rub, groan, rub, groan.

Mr. H. had a Victrola, one of the earliest models, with a crank, a long horn, and a picture on it of a hound listening to a Victrola which had a picture on it of a hound listening to a Victrola. Over and above the counterpoint of chopping, washing, scrubbing and groaning could be heard the penetrating voice of Enrico Caruso breaking into the tragic laugh of Pagliacci over and over and over again, a laugh which seemed to have something to say about the lives of these people. From Mr. H. we learned such household words as Mishelman (Mischa Elman), Gallikoortchie (Galli-Curci), and Hayfitz (Jascha Heifetz). The older men would gather before Mr. H's Victrola and sway from side to side in religious ecstasy, carried away by the heavenly tones of some great cantor.

There were the unconquerables like Mrs. N., who converted a dark tenement apartment into an enchanted palace, lighted exclusively from within. She scrubbed her pots to a high finish and hung them like mirrors around the kitchen wall. Her coal stove was polished to an ebony luster. Whatever light managed to get through the windows was dimmed by stiffly starched curtains. Her children wore freshly ironed dresses and patent-leather shoes. We weren't allowed to play in her house because we "made dirt."

Mrs. L. was years ahead of the other women. She *owned* a thermometer, and in her house they ate lettuce. The other neighbors said that lettuce was for cows. Her kids got milk of magnesia instead of castor oil. She even sent her wash to the laundry. This was going too far! The other women remarked that no genuine housewife would send her things to the laundry "to tear them to pieces."

Mrs. B. was always "in the middle of a cake." She shuffled about in house slippers and was never seen without a dripping ladle in one hand and a feather bread-lacquering brush in the other. She invariably forgot to turn off her gas stove but she never smelled anything. She moved about in a semicoma and was always surprised when we came to rescue her. She blamed her headaches on her husband.

❀❀❀❀❀

One of the principal services the women performed was getting each other's daughters married. Only a bachelor with long years of experience as a fugitive from matrimony could escape marrying one of the girls in our building. The vigilante mothers of marriageable daughters captured more men than the FBI. They didn't doubt that marriages were made in Heaven, but they knew that unless they moved Heaven and earth, Clara second floor back just wasn't gonna make it.

Their strategy was ingenious and revealed a sailor's familiarity with knot tying. A family with an "available" girl never moved into a building where there were no "possibles." Hot food (Plan A) was the brain softener. When a "possible" was expected for a visit, the kitchen went on a double shift. They packed so much food into the prospect's mouth that if he tried to say No he'd choke to death. I saw many a victim stagger down the aisle under the influence of chicken soup. The warm glow he felt, though somewhat akin to passion, was only its first cousin —heartburn.

While there was no time for tryouts in Philadelphia, the scene was acted out with theatrical perfection. Once the food was in the "possible," neighbors and friends dropped in to say hello. Within the first hour a rumor had spread that they were engaged. The second string of neighbors dropped in to congratulate the girl's mother. Latecomers already referred to him as "the son-in-law."

Plan B (for nonresident "possibles") worked as follows: "I'll invite my nephew over for supper, then your Bernice will step in at about nine o'clock to return the nasal drops which I loaned you, and I will introduce them to each other. I'll ask Bernice to have tea with us. I know that once he sees her half the battle is over."

No matter how few and feeble the virtues of the girl, she was perfection itself according to the "pitch." If she was short and weighed two hundred pounds, she was petite and plump. If she was homely they'd say, "Wait till you hear her play the piano." And if the girl was indisputably ugly she was declared to be "very intelligent."

When any of the girls in our building acquired a "steady," all the neighbors began to make inquiries of her mother. This was a test case of how well a girl from a tenement could do.

"Is he a nice fellow?"

"What does he do for a living?"

If he wasn't "making a nice dollar" there was one alternative that was completely acceptable to the mothers. Learning power was admired even more than earning power—"He's studying." A girl who was "going" with a student could keep "going" for a long time. "He'll be all right. He's for her and she's for him. God willing, may my Dorothy make a catch like Gertrude's."

If *our* Ruthie from *our* building was getting married, her mother went from door to door: "Come and help us celebrate." Even toothless babies in their carriages munched honey cake. The women ran in and out of the bride's apartment with scissors, ribbons, and combs in their hands. Heated arguments developed over her hairdo. "Not like that! She looks twenty years older. The hair should be over the ears, not under. You don't need so many bows in the back."

Some of the neighbors stood around the stoop trying to identify the wedding guests as they arrived: "That's her Uncle Arnold from Passaic, and that's his second wife. That one I don't know. Must be from his side. They are very ritzy people. They're in paper boxes. Here come the flowers." Western Union messengers were directed by the kids: "Third floor back."

"He's coming!" A taxi pulled up at the door. First to

come out were the groom's parents, then the young man in a high hat and frock coat. He strode through with a severity unbecoming his youthful, rosy-cheeked countenance, ignoring the crowd of first-nighters.

Minutes later two five-year old scouts came rushing down the stairs screaming "She's coming!" The echo ran through the crowd. "She's coming, she's coming." She came. No longer "Ruthie third floor back," but a vision of loveliness in white. The women cried and the kids sang, "Here comes the bride, all dressed in white; here comes the feller, all dressed in yeller."

As a reward for their efforts the neighbors were invited to the wedding, where over the roast chicken they whispered to each other, "Between me and you, he's not for her, and she's not for him."

❊❊❊❊❊

Somewhere between neighbor and relative there existed the ambiguous category of boarder—a sleep-in stranger who might stay from a week to forty years. He had the impersonal, nondescript face one sees in the newspapers as "the artist's composite picture of the criminal."

The boarder was usually an asexual type who had the same relationship to the lady of the house as the porter in a convent has to the mother superior. (It often happened, though, that an unemployed boarder with time on his hands became the other man in a drama played behind closed doors and windows, yet loud enough for all the neighbors to follow without a program.)

Even though he walked around the house in his underwear, the boarder was still respectfully referred to as *Mr. Fliggel*. He became part of the family. Whatever money he could save was deposited with "the Mrs." whom he trusted as though she were his mother. Mornings, he had top priority in the use of the bathroom, and evenings he could sit and look out of the window undisturbed for as long as he liked.

The letter boxes downstairs rarely listed only the family name. Apt. 4B accepted mail for Freeman, Hausman, Marks, Moss and Tepper. This was one place where even the Royal Canadian Mounted Police could never find their man. The usual answer to a man with a summons was "He moved." The boarder had earned this protection because there were times when he was the only one in the family who was working. If he was a dress operator, he sewed things for the girls. There were many instances when the boarder paid for Fanny's piano lessons or bought Davie a pair of shoes for the holidays. When there was a fire in a building the boarders were rescued first, then came women and children, the rubber plant, and finally the fathers.

Boarders were a great subject for gossip and rumor. There were some facts we were sure of: he slept in a long nightgown; he was tattooed; he kept raw eggs in his dresser; he bought razor blades a thousand for nineteen cents; he sent poems to newspapers and read political pamphlets. The rest was rumor: he was a deserter from the Kaiser's army; he wore a money belt; he had two wives in Passaic, New Jersey; he was inventing a substitute for plaster.

The "Mrs." was always sorry for him, much to her

husband's disgust. "Poor man," she'd say, "he's all alone in the world—no family." To which her husband would usually mutter, "I'll change places with him any time."

❀❀❀❀❀

From the children's point of view it was hard to tell a neighbor from a relative. "She's like a sister to me" was said in all sincerity. Door-to-door living over long periods of time made these people true kin to each other. The only difference between neighbors and relatives was that the neighbors went home to sleep; the relatives could climb into bed with you.

There was no such thing as unexpected company. Mama was always expecting. Every day brought an additional boatload of poor, hungry immigrants to these shores. Each immigrant in turn missed an occasional meal so that he might send for some dear one left behind.

They all landed in our house, where every room became a guest room, every bed a guest bed, and every kid a host. As children we learned perforce to share time and space with others.

They sat around our table, drank steaming hot tea, and told and retold their stories. In the great oral tradition of history, they traced the annals of our family down to the last remembered incidents, imbuing me with a feeling of historical continuity.

I was fascinated by their collective and individual adventures, their fortunes and misfortunes. They told of our great-great-grandfather who had had four wives, from one or another of which we had descended; how the parents and grandparents had built houses near each other and raised their children together; of plagues and children (some with my name) who had died in them; of hiding in cellars during pogroms; of marriages arranged by parents and of some rebellious flights from them; of miracle-working rabbis; of drunken Cossacks invading their homes; of anti-Czarist meetings in the woods, arrests, sentences to Siberia and escapes to America; of hysterical reunions of brothers each of whom had thought the other was dead. Theirs was a great saga and I was part of it.

As I grew older I came to realize that this family also had all the less than heroic qualities of all families. Even the best of families are divided, as was ours, into two factions, Mama's side and Papa's side, referred to by the opposite number as "they," "them," "his people," "her people," "that gang," or simply "you know who."

As kids we knew who were the "good guys" and who the "bad guys," but we also knew better than to take sides. As brother David used to say, "Either side is suicide." Mama could make some snide remark, as could Papa, but if one of the kids ever repeated what he had heard Mama say he was told to show a little more respect.

"They're all alike to me," Mama would say. "It's all one big family." However, if somebody from Papa's side dropped in, Mama would mumble, "He's here already, or again, or still, or for a change." If, on the other hand, somebody from Mama's side happened to show up un-expectedly at 3 A.M. in a snowstorm, Mama would clasp her hands to her bosom and say, "You see? Blood is not water. A relative is a relative after all. He came to see me!"

If somebody from Mama's side ate us out of house and

home, Mama used to say, "God bless him! He's got such a
hearty appetite! It's a pleasure to feed him!" If somebody
from Papa's side did the same thing, Mama said, "A
regular garbage can!"

There were ways of handling the family dichotomy to
advantage. If you had a party and didn't want cousin A.
to come, you told her that Uncle B. would be there. If
you didn't want Aunt C., you said that Uncle D. would
be there. In fact, if you invited everybody, nobody came.
Some of the uncles weren't on the best of terms with
certain other uncles whose wives were friendly only with
certain preferred sisters-in-law who knew "the truth"
about certain cousins. Those who weren't invited ra-
tionalized: "So they won't have the pleasure of our company. They don't deserve the happiness we would bring
to the affair." There were some relatives who would show
up invited or not invited: "I came to show you I wasn't
angry because you forgot to invite me."

Our family had a legendary rich uncle in California.
He went West immediately upon arriving in this country
and wasn't heard of for decades, but stories drifted back
to the East. "Uncle Charlie? A millionaire! One millionaire? Two millionaires! Lives in a mansion with thirty-
two male servants, fifteen thousand head of cattle, eleven
children, all sons, each one a millionaire. He's connected
with the Government, the movies, Wall Street."

Each one of our poor Eastern uncles had said at some
time in his life, "If I had listened to Uncle Charlie, I
wouldn't be where I am today." And each poor Eastern
aunt had thought aloud, "If I had the sense to marry
Uncle Charlie, I wouldn't be standing here over a wash-

tub. I'd be sitting out there, next to my own little oil well not far from my seltzer fountain, in my own orange grove behind my movie studio next to my railroad."

After many years of silence a letter came from "Diamond Charlie." Why hadn't we written? Send someone at once to the land of milk and honey. So the family shipped off Uncle Boris, who, in turn, promised to arrange a mass exodus of all the relatives, each to his private paradise. Uncle Boris came back six weeks later with a healthy suntan and without four hundred dollars, which the fabulous uncle had "invested" for the relatives. No more letters came. The legend died. Uncle Charlie, as any one of the uncles would tell you, was a good-for-nothing even in the old country—"May his oil well explode and burn down his mansion and his orange grove and his railroad."

To counterbalance our rich uncle in California we had a poor but "influential" uncle in the East. He knew people; he had "connections." Some of the relatives said "he couldn't get you arrested," but he could, and did. If he couldn't get you into West Point he could get you a PFC at Western Union. He could also get you jury duty, a birth certificate, or a free chest X-ray at the Board of Health. If you were in real trouble he gave you his confidential list of people to borrow from.

Then there was Uncle D., the anticapitalist whom the family was always setting up in business. The first time it cost them a fortune to keep him going for a year; then he failed. The next time he saved the family thousands of dollars by failing immediately. To complicate his life and ours even more, he was a political agitator who saw no point in seeking permanent employment in a social order which was going to be liquidated at any moment.

Papa had a sort of cousin who always sort of happened to be in the neighborhood at mealtime. We used to say, "Let's try eating early. Maybe he'll come late." No use. We would invite him to join us. "No, thank you," he would say. "I'm not hungry. I just had a big meal at home. Maybe I'll just have a little nibble with you." Papa couldn't take it. "Look, cousin. I'm not a rich man. Maybe you could arrange to eat with us and nibble at home." We called him "Cousin Nibble, the poor eater." The other uncles used him as a pointer, so that occasionally the whole starved pack would descend on us. If the wind was right (even in the winter when the windows were closed) he could sniff chicken soup five blocks away and tell whether it had noodles. To him anything hot "smelled delicious"—coal, gas, or a burning building.

There were the quarreling aunt and uncle who never arrived together. "Where's Aunt N.?" "She's coming, she coming." They were the perfect mismatch. He was short and she was tall; he was fast and she was slow; he was healthy and she was sick. They couldn't travel together. He couldn't ride forward and she couldn't ride backward and they couldn't possibly face each other. They had six children and twenty grandchildren, and they never talked to each other.

We had the standard assortment of colorful aunts, too—the Fainter, who was always slipping off her chair unnoticed; the Town Crier, who wept whether the news was good or bad; the Drafty Aunt who always felt a breeze on her neck. The latter would shudder and ask for someone to please close the window. I remember when she complained of a draft on the boardwalk at Coney Island.

There was one aunt who was so old she had forgotten

who she was, and there was no living relative who could remember. Even her husband wasn't quite sure who she was. My brothers started a rumor that their marriage license had expired and they were living in sin. She used to pet the newborn babies and say, "He looks like his great-grandfather, Uncle Z." Who could check on it?

Aunt B. had been courted by Cousin Z. when she was a young girl. She turned him down because he had tried to hold her hand. Who knows what that kind of man might pull later? He moved to California to forget. She stayed home and thought it over. Forty years later she got in touch with him and offered to forgive and forget and marry him. He died exactly one day before she arrived. She took it badly, realizing that she might have been married all those years to a very nice man. Since she was already in California, she married another man. He died three years later leaving her with a cabinet full of unused medicine. She married once again. He died. She then came back to New York, where she resumed her life as a single girl.

Our relatives were almost without exception working people whose occupation became part of their identification: Nathan the butcher, Sam the painter, Annie the bastings-puller. They had gone to work as young children. Their poverty had cut their childhood short and aborted their talents.

Mama never talked about it, but her contemporaries often told me that when she was a young girl (in itself almost inconceivable to me) she had an unusually beautiful voice. I remember Mama singing a great deal in the kitchen in a tired, breathless, hopeless, echoless voice that seemed ideally suited to the sad songs she sang. Her favorite was "The Prisoner's Song"—"If I had the wings of an angel, over these prison walls I would fly." Small wonder that she drove me on to practice the violin. "I never had the chance. You!" And she enjoyed my playing, which was sad enough.

Aunt C. lived by herself in a dark basement after her husband died, almost all the rest of her life, but she was never alone. She had a zither and a broken-down piano, and while the potato pancakes were frying she would plunk out some bizarre air of her own creation, as out of tune with life as she herself was. The mice came out to listen. Apparently she had something in common with her audience, which also lived in the shadows.

Her husband, Uncle H., had been a house painter, and also an artist in his own right. No ordinary painter could come up with such lyrical murals—sailboats on a deep blue sea against a dying red sun; and such clouds—little bundles of absorbent cotton suspended in the heavens, and Dutch windmills, and flowing brooks, and timid lions peering through the brush, and princesses with parasols, and small trees that looked like asparagus stalks—a Brooklyn Rousseau. If he had lived longer he might have achieved some recognition, but his wife's burning potato pancakes ruined his lungs. The doctor said it was the lead in the paint. We knew better.

At least half a dozen aunts could have been sculptors. They would shape dough into the most delightful patterns. Their baking had design and a wealth of artistic imagination. An ordinary white bread was topped with strips of dough braided into chains that criss-crossed each other. A cooky was shaped into a flower, an animal, a fish, a walking cane, a star, or a moonface with raisins for eyes. They looked, and sometimes even tasted, like pottery.

Uncle Elias was born to be an engineer. For him, fixing a dripping faucet was a creative experience. He never bought a part. He preferred to manufacture his own. He could make a washer out of a checker. He made stuck windows slide up and down by using a secret formula: Vaseline. He silenced knocking radiators by inserting a pin in some secret place. He resuscitated dead radio sets by connecting a wire to a disconnected radiator. I saw him restore life to an electric iron by a delicate piece of safety-pin heart surgery.

When he was still a young man, the doctor advised him to have an operation on his nose so he could breathe. He looked at the doctor condescendingly. When he got home he devised a contraption consisting of two cardboard tubes which he inserted into his nose at bedtime, permitting him to breathe all night up to the age of eighty. Had he been able to do something equally helpful for his heart, he would still be around today.

❈❈❈❈❈

Although there were eight of us children, we were outnumbered by two parents. Ours was a decidedly parent-centered home. Since respect for age was a cornerstone of our tradition, it followed that Mama and Papa had the right to lead, and we had the right to be led by them. We had very few other rights. We had lots of wrongs which were going to be corrected by any methods our parents saw fit. The last thought that would have entered my parents' minds was to ask their children what was good or bad for children. We were not their contemporaries, nor their equals, and they were not concerned with our ideas on how to raise a family. "When I need your opinion I'll give it to you."

We had to wait our turn to speak our minds. It was not clear to us when that turn would come, but I knew that I would have to become a little older and a little wiser before I would be called in as a consultant by my parents. If I offered a suggestion, Mama would say, "Wait. Papa is talking." When I got to be thirteen (Bar Mitzvah and manhood), I took a chance. "Now, Ma?"

"Not yet."

Most things were "none of my business"—even when they were talking about having my tonsils out. I got the idea finally that my mind was to be used to mind: to mind Papa, mind your teacher, mind your manners, mind your shoes. My shoes were my brother's, my hat was my father's, my bed was anybody's, so I didn't really feel entitled to a mind of my own.

On the walls there were hand-embroidered maxims: Silence Is Golden; Hear No Evil, Speak No Evil, See No Evil; Empty Barrels Make the Most Noise; Dogs Carry Tales; Talk Is Cheap. It all boiled down to a house policy of "Who Asked You?"

They did not have to explain the basis for their actions, nor did they say, "This hurts me more than it hurts you." If you pressed them for a reason they quoted some authority known as "Because!" If Mama said No to something I wanted to do, and I used the argument that "Louie is doing it, and Georgie is doing it, and Benny . . ." she would cut in with "When I tell you No, don't tell me Who."

They did everything the psychologists today condemn. They humiliated us ("A boy your age should know better"); they belittled us ("Look who's talking"); they reminded us of their sacrifices on our behalf ("This is my reward!") ; they raised their voices at us ("Now do you hear me?"); or, what was still worse, Mama gave us the silent treatment. She wouldn't talk to us for days, and no matter how hard we tried to make up, our terms were not acceptable.

Mama believed, or pretended to believe, that anything her kids could do someone else's kids could do better.

"Ma! I got promoted to the fifth grade today!"

"So what? Georgie upstairs is in the eighth grade."

One day I put all my good deeds in one basket in a deliberate attempt to stun her by a display of dazzling virtue. I went to the store, helped set the table, served the food, washed the dishes, and swept the dining room. That evening I hung around fishing for a compliment. "I helped you tonight, didn't I, Mama?"

And Mama said, "You ate, didn't you?"

Nor did they hesitate to revive previous offenses. "And how about the time you spilled the ink on the tablecloth? And how about the time you stuck out the eyes on Grandpa's picture? . . ."

My parents' attitude was "Better that the neighbors should say nice things about our children than we should." They believed that to compliment a child was to spoil him. Perhaps they felt they were placing our eternal souls in jeopardy by indulging themselves or us in the sin of pride.

There were also comparisons made with anonymous kids who belonged to that perfect species known as "Other People's Children." Other people's children were clean, helpful, respectful, intelligent, and you weren't ashamed to take them places. We were dirty, helpless, disrespectful, unintelligent, and they were ashamed to take us anywhere.

We sometimes suffered comparisons with dumb animals. "Even a dog stands up when company comes into the room." "Even a cat washes his face before dinner."

Papa frequently used the "when I was your age" technique. When he was a boy he was older and stronger and smarter than any of us. He was quite a prodigy, to judge by his alleged childhood achievements. When he was my age he had a wife and six children, supported his aged parents, and earned the equivalent of a hundred and fifty American dollars a week while starving in a damp cellar.

"When are you going to start acting like a man?" was Papa's eternal query, even to my sister.

My folks knew nothing about child psychology as we understand it today, but they knew plenty about the workings of the mind of a child. They could slyly maneuver you into a *fait accompli:* "Sammy, I think I saw a penny on the sidewalk in front of the butcher store. On the way home from the butcher store you'll pick up a dozen eggs." Before I had time to realize I was being sent on an errand, I was home with the eggs and no penny.

If there was a mob of noisy kids in the house Mama would announce, "Whoever goes home first gets a cooky."

If you wanted a toy, Mama might say, "A big boy like you! Toys are for children." (What child would admit he was a child?)

If I hit Harold, "Is this the first time you hit Harold?" Either way I answered that question I was guilty.

If you wanted something that Papa couldn't afford to give you, he refused not on grounds of poverty but because it wasn't good for you. For roller skates: "You might run into a truck and get killed." For going to the movies: "The sunshine is better for you." For money: "You'll only spend it"—or he got conveniently hard of hearing: "Give me a nickel." "A pickle?" "No, Pa, money, a nickel." "A honey pickle?" "I want to buy an ice-cream cone." "Take a bath; it'll cool you off better." A new suit: "To me you're beautiful just as you are."

It is not as difficult as it seems to explain the common use of corporal punishment in those days. Anything animate or inanimate, that did not respond to reason was hit with the palm of the hand: gas burners, radio, drawers, windows or children. With the latter a combination of couch therapy and corporal punishment worked best. The kid was told to stretch out on the lounge. He then pulled down his pants and "voluntarily" exposed his psyche for the shock treatment. Most of the time we got only token punishments—small pinches, twists and pokes.

It was possible to be spanked unjustly. Life is that way. If you protested that you "didn't do nothing," Papa still did not apologize. "O.K. So that's for what you did that I didn't know about." If one of us committed an offense, we all got hit on the theory that we were all accessories, if not by direct participation, then by a conspiracy of silence.

If two brothers got into a fight Mama would arbitrate. She would bring the two conflicting parties together, explain that such behavior was a sin against God and man. Then, when she thought we finally understood, she banged our heads together to leave a lasting impression on our minds.

Did we end up hating our parents? No. Why? Because we understood the dogma involved. It was the dogma of parental responsibility, of preventive therapy, of virtue being its own reward and evil bringing punishment. Did we enjoy the practice? Of course not. We understood that a world as tough as ours required tough parents and tough teachers. They had to fight fire with fire. The fight against individual corruption was part of the fight against the environment. The moral standard of the home had to be higher than that of the street. "You are not on the street; you are in our home. This is not a cellar nor a poolroom. Here we act like human beings, not like animals." I remember the speech well. Like royalty, Mama said "we." "We have been put to shame by what you did." Did it make me feel guilty? It sure did. Did I feel I had let the family down? I sure did. Was it worth a quick sharp pain in the rear end to be reminded of my obligations? It sure was. Better one stabbing moment of truth at home than a stabbing in the street.

One thing was sure. In our home we knew the House Rules. They were:

1. Respect was to be shown all elders.

2. There was no such thing as a petty crime. Little offenses can lead to big ones. Practice makes perfect.

3. The management reserved the right to screen your friends.

4. When the sun set you came home.

5. You had to earn good marks in school or money, or both. Loafing was out and unearned money was suspect.

6. You could be a hero in your own home. Try it. (Papa was, Mama was, and so was any one who brought honor to the family.)

❀❀❀❀❀

I was about twelve years old when it was decided to leave the old tenement and move to a better apartment in Brooklyn—the suburbs. Sister Dora was already married and living there, and Joe, Jack and David were married, too. All felt it would be easier for Mama. Mama put up a fight against the move. She quoted an old proverb: "To a worm in horseradish, the horseradish seems sweet." She came up with a set of arguments against progress:

1. "You can't bake a decent cake in a gas range, only in a coal stove. Coal gives the healthiest heat. And what am I going to do with all the stove polish? Throw it out?"

2. "From steam heat you get sinus trouble, radiators knock and keep you up all night, and boilers explode. I read in the paper about a mother and eight children— blown to pieces."

3. "Here we have a nice fire escape and a roof. In Brooklyn where will the children play? In the yard? They can get hurt there. I read in the papers . . ."

4. "Brooklyn is full of cemeteries. So you can't wait for me to close my eyes. Such children! Tell the truth! The doctor told you to take me to Brooklyn? Now I understand. Soon you'll read in the papers . . ."

I shall never forget Mama's anguish as she watched

each piece of furniture being carried out of the apartment, parts of our lives plucked up indifferently by strange men and thrown onto a truck. What used to be a home was before her eyes becoming just a house again, and the scenes of our family history just rooms. As she moved about from room to room she relived these scenes. Right here next to this faded wallpaper was where Sammy had had pneumonia, and this was the room where Jack and Joe had studied for so many years. A room once filled with so much hope and driving ambition would soon be occupied by strangers who wouldn't even care. Jack had married Florence in this same front room where in the summer time the boys had made an orchestra, Jack on the fiddle, David, Mike and Joe mandolins, Bill on the uke, and Al and myself as the enthusiastic apprentices. The sudden transition from the familiar past into the unpredictable future was too much for Mama. She raised the window and looked out into the damp, dark courtyard and did what she always did when under great emotional stress. She talked to herself: "Where am I going to? What am I lacking here? So many good, loyal friends, to leave them all behind. Why? Let me remain here."

Mama was the last one to leave the apartment. As a final gesture of respect for her old home she washed the floors.

When we got downstairs the women were all waiting. Some turned their faces away, others wept unashamedly. "Good luck! Good luck! May it all be for the best. Be well, and may your children bring you joy."

II
"Look, Ma, I'm middle class!"

✲✲✲✲✲

B‌Y THE TIME my wife and I got around to establishing a family of our own, the institution of home had been remodeled almost beyond recognition. Mama's and Papa's old family order had fallen into disrepute. At best it was patronized as quaint; at worst it was looked upon as representing an age of psychological ignorance, domestic bondage, parental tyranny and emotional repression.

Like most other young couples, we moved away from the old neighborhood, away from Mama, away from her skirt into the outskirts. The new housing developments were located symbolically and geographically next door to the cemeteries of Mama's generation, communities without signposts, roads or traditions.

Everything that was "new" was good, because it belonged to the "enlightened" way. Yesterday's values had to be jettisoned merely because they were yesterday's. We were now living in a great testing laboratory in which hypotheses were enthusiastically and prematurely declared to be truths. Instant tradition was being brewed up in a pressure cooker, and the steam was hitting us in the eyes. A new canon, hypercritical of everything but itself, took possession of our lives, prescribing new customs, new fanaticisms, new intolerances and new clichés.

Everybody and everything had been emancipated in a sort of general amnesty, and freedom took off in all directions.

Women's rights were extended from the kitchen into the bedroom; fidelity became optional; sex went on the stage; obscenity became literary honesty; ritual became a spectator sport; science became a religion; religious holidays became days off; homemaking became interior decoration; informality became compulsory; ugly became interesting; patriotism became suspect; furniture became uncomfortable; poetry became incomprehensible; knitting became therapy; abnormal became normal; love became biology; paintings became Rorschach tests; psychology became a gospel; guilt became corporate; punishment became a crime; fathers became pals and the children became the ruling class of a new tribal order, the Kindergarchy—government by the kids, of the kids, for the kids, with the parents retained as unpaid servants, permitted to answer the phone, take messages, and in some cases to eat with the children.

Having had the good fortune to have lived before, during and after this revolution, I am in a position to compare the old and new family mores:

THE OLD

1. A home smelled like no other place in the world. Every breath of life you drew there contained particles of Essence of Home, a strong perfume blended of soup, soap,

THE NEW

1. The modern home is expected to smell like an eighteenth-century boudoir, an effect achieved by spraying compressed seduction out of a can.

brothers, beds, liniment, furniture polish, hair tonic, gym shoes and other exotica domestica.

2. You went to school; the school didn't come for you. (You probably also noticed that the older you got the longer was your walk to school.)

2. The mother drives the child to the corner and keeps his body warm in the car until the bus picks him up. If the child ever smelled fresh air he'd get the bends. For this child, gasoline fumes will some day bring back memories of school days.

3. When the child came home from school Mama asked two questions:
a. "Were you a good boy?"
b. "What did you learn today?"

3. The streamlined mother asks only one question: "Were you happy in school today?" Yes. He was happy. The teacher is still in a coma, but this little man has had a happy day. Any child who is not happy can get a divorce from his teacher.

4. If Mama thought you had misbehaved she could punish you in several ways:
a. A spanking
b. Revocation of some privilege
c. Court-martial in front of the entire family
d. Ostracism until you seemed fully repentant

4. The mother punishes herself for her incompetence in parent-child relationships, admits to the child that it was her fault, then consults a psychiatrist to find out why the child "rejects" her.

5. Mama taught her daughter to dress modestly, be reticent and virtuous. Prince Charming would come along, sooner or later.

5. Mother now teaches her daughter how to use make-up seductively, presents her with a road map of the best places to find a man, and provides

THE OLD

THE NEW

her with the latest information on antidotes for the population explosion to keep her out of trouble until Prince Charming comes along.

6. It took a girl about three years after the arrival of Prince Charming to get married:
Flirting—two months
Holding hands—three months
First kiss—after six months
House calls—six months
Family approval—one year of investigation of his ancestry, finances, intentions and character.
Planning the wedding—at least one year of meetings of tribal chieftains.

6. "Look, darling, if you like him that's all that matters. All I ask is caterer's rights, two free passes for Daddy and me, and the privilege of paying your way through college. If the baby comes before that it can live with us until you get your degree."

7. *Nobody* got an allowance. There was a cracked teapot in the cupboard that contained the family money for the week. If any one needed any part of it he petitioned Mama, the treasurer, "I *need* six cents." Papa could announce, "I'm *taking* thirty cents," but no one else could take without asking.

7. The four-year-old lawyer who lives next door has advised your child that he is "entitled" to an allowance, or minimum wage for living at home. An intelligent parent will see to it that this payoff will match equivalent standards in other communities on the same socioeconomic level.

8. A child could be ordered to go to the grocery store right away and get two quarts of milk, come back right away and not sip from the milk can.

8. The parents must inquire as to the child's availability. "If you don't mind, Georgie, on the way back from the Little League game,

if it isn't too much of an effort, and you happen to be coming home, would you mind . . . ?" (By the way, this is *his* dinner you're talking about.)

9. A bad report card could mean many things. The child was:
a. Lazy
b. Inattentive
c. Bad
d. Not very bright
e. Just like his father
(All of these conditions would have to be remedied by the child.)

9. A bad report card means simply that the teacher does not appreciate the gifts of your child. The teacher is:
a. Lazy
b. Inattentive
c. Bad
d. Not very bright
e. Just like the principal
(All of these conditions will have to be remedied by the teacher.)

10. Mama visited the school only when sent for.

10. Mother's attendance at the school is better than the kid's. If the mother is absent they send for the child.

11. No one sat down at the table for dinner until the father was seated. He was served first, then the oldest child, then down the line to the baby, and no one left the table until dinner was over.

11. The kids are fed first and gotten out of the way so the parents can eat the leftovers in peace.

12. The children learned to eat by imitation. They picked up the basic uses for a fork and knife early—the fork for nailing down the food and the knife for protecting it from marauders. If the meat

12. The child's food is mashed, smashed, squashed, ground, filtered, homogenized, served on dishes shaped like windmills, turtles, bears, imprinted with nursery rhymes and puzzles. Children's food

THE OLD

was tough it was tough on everybody. Papa told you it was even tougher if you didn't have any.

13. After dinner the dining-room table was cleared off and the children sat down to do their homework.

14. Mama was one up on the genie of Aladdin's lamp. You didn't need a lamp to summon her. She was always present whether you rubbed her the right way or the wrong way. You could stand on a mountain peak and yell "Hey, Ma," and the echo would come back, "What now?"

15. Mama was the original do-it-yourselfer. She selected a chicken, plucked it, cleaned it, cooked it, and used up

THE NEW

must crackle, pop, whistle, talk, sing, and be eaten with itsy-bitsy spoons in itsy-bitsy portions up to graduation from high school. In college the house mother has to cut up the meat for the freshman class.

13. The parent sets aside some nice quiet place for homework, then sits down and does it for the child. This will leave the child time to pursue his other interests, such as watching TV, staring, moping, head-scratching and telephoning.

14. Today's child also knows where his mother is. All he has to do is to read the note on the family bulletin board: "Darling—If I'm not at the PTA, or the Save the Children Luncheon, or the Homemakers' Meeting, I'll be at the hairdresser's. Start defrosting at four. If I'm not home by five start joyful family living together without me. Your loving mother, Mary Harrington, B.A. M.A., cum laude."

15. Today, thank heaven, we don't have to do anything for ourselves. Everything is pre-prepared, presliced, pre-

every last part down to the feathers, which were cleaned and stuffed into quilts.

16. The living room was used for living.

17. People came to see people.

cooked, preheated, prefabricated, premixed, prefrozen, prewhipped, premashed, prediced, preshrunk, presteamed and pretested—so how come we are all so tired at night?

16. The living-room furniture must be protected from the living. The children's hands are grimy and Grandma's elastic stockings catch on the threads of the brocaded ottoman. So, everybody, out! —to the den or the playroom. The living room is sealed off and the upholstery allowed to fade in peace.

17. We are back in the Dark Ages: The lights are out and the television set is on. There are shadows eating peanuts and drinking beer. The answer to "Good evening" is "Shhh!" At eleven the lights are turned on, everybody says "Hello," and goes home.

The children who have "made it" seek to share the joys of the "rich" environment with Mama, to repay her for the years of self-denial on their behalf. She is uprooted and transplanted bodily to the suburbs where she lives in retirement, a D.P. living in comfort with her children. She now has her own room, her own foam-rubber mattress, her own TV set, her own parakeet, and youthful shoes. Her new environment does not reflect her in any way. The old "corny" photographs of relatives have been taken off the walls and replaced by abstract paintings of the artist's conception of the artist's mother. For Mama this home is a stage set, well-appointed but unreal. She tries to act out the part of Dowager Queen, but her performance does not quite come off. She is discomfited by all this comfort.

She cannot articulate her loneliness. In fact, she must not, for fear of being declared ungrateful. She has forfeited a basic human right—the right to complain.

"Granny" is taken to fancy luncheons in stylish clothes. "How can you tell a Sabbath or a holiday from all other days if you are dressed up all the time?" When visitors come, she puts on ribbons and sits in the corner of the room, an expensive, gift-wrapped, empty box.

The children cannot understand Grandma's joylessness. In spite of the fact that she now has "everything," Grandma doesn't want and doesn't need everything. She doesn't want servants; she wants to serve. She doesn't want a ready-made home. She wants one for which she can shop, chop, grind, perspire, work and give. She doesn't want to be a status symbol for her successful children. Quiet and lawns do not "send" her. People and sidewalks are what she wants. She wants to meet people by accident rather than by invitation.

She cannot understand why her children who have such beautiful homes, are always going someplace. She doesn't like to be taken out to restaurants to eat food she could prepare better and less expensively at home. She certainly doesn't need a "combo" playing in the background.

As an unaccredited authority on family life she considers her daughter's "professional" rearing of her children as unnatural and says so. "Never mind what 'they' say. I'm telling you. Who is 'they'? I raised eight children and never had a 'they.' Broiled chicken is healthy; but mine you never forgot, right?" When her daughter throws a party, Mama is requested to make one dish in the old style so the sophisticated crowd can go slumming at home.

If the family moves to a "smart" apartment house instead a home in the suburbs Mama makes friends with the underground—the maids, the elevator man, the doorman and the janitor. They bring her news from "there." At the peak of success she feels deprived, and she mumbles something about "Man does not live by bread alone."

❦❦❦❦❦

Mama had eight kids and no theories. My wife and I were blessed with two kids and eight hundred theories beamed at us every day, all day, from magazines, radio and TV programs, diaper-service bulletins, books, pamphlets, checklists, progress charts, authorities, authorities, authorities.

What most of the "experts" told us, in essence, was that our dear Mama was nothing but a germ-carrying, highly emotional carnivore who devoured the egos of her children. We were warned to keep our offspring out of her reach. What they didn't tell us was that it was easier on Mama's nervous system to raise her kids than it is for the overadvised young mother of this era.

There are about four hundred books on child care

published each year. Unfortunately the latest book very often contradicts the next to the latest by the same author who in the interim has also read a book.

The bewildered mother loses faith in her maternal instincts. She becomes "outer-directed." The fear of doctrinal error paralyzes her. She has gone from economic insecurity in her mother's home to emotional insecurity in her own. "Am I adequate?" "Am I giving too much, expecting too much, too little? Am I mothering or smothering, overprotecting or underprotecting, overconcerned or underconcerned, obsessive, repressive?" The natural joy of caring for her babies is destroyed by the dread of making the wrong decision. Love must be sterilized and defined before it can be used. Love is "an emotional experience involving a slight increase in body temperature, hyperactivity of the pituitary glands, and a loss of blood supply to the brain." A mother is "a female mammal, not necessarily of the human race, one who has generated offspring through the voluntary or involuntary assistance of an agent of the opposite sex, generally referred to as the male." A kiss is "the juxtaposition of the fleshy folds surrounding the orifice of the mouth accompanied by irregular stifled breathing through the nose."

Mama believed that caressing fingers run through a child's hair also smooth the wrinkles out of his psyche, that a kiss on the injured spot does "make it better," that children love those who love them, that conflicts between mothers and children, like lovers' quarrels, are soon patched up, that love comes with a built-in tolerance for error.

It is not easy for the mother to accept the premise that whatever goes wrong with the child's mental life is her

fault. The child is infallible; she is not. She must count
her words and police her own behavior at all times. She
must always remain calm and reasonable, never, under
any conditions, raising her voice. If she must let off steam
she can go into the bathroom and scream at the turtle. To
protect the child's mind she may have to lose her own.
One false move, however innocent, and she's got a problem child on her hands. He sucks his thumb because of
something she did or did not say, suggest, or imply. He
sneezes, coughs, wets, winks, belches, falls, eats, or doesn't
eat because of something *she* did or did not do.

Did she make him ashamed of anything? This must
never happen. Enlightened parents know, for example,
that the use of four-letter words by a child is a passing
phase (two months to thirty-seven years) and is best left
unnoticed. This is a little difficult when you have a
house full of unenlightened guests who *do* notice and
expect you to do something about it.

One thing has been made pretty clear to us by the dirt
specialists: Don't suppress four-letter words or they will
multiply in the subconscious into eight- and sixteen-letter
words which are much harder to handle (and to spell).
It is only a question of whether your patience will give
out before the "phase" does. The father's endurance
usually breaks down first and he will shout: "Where in
H—— does the little ——— pick up such language?"
This outburst is good for the child since he now realizes
that his father is going through the same phase. Incidentally, the worst stage a kid ever goes through is the one
he is going through right now.

The young mother should be told during her pregnancy
what to expect of a normal child so she won't go out of

her mind later wondering whether she has given birth to a fiend. She should be forewarned that these are the things a normal child does, not because his mommy said or did anything to crush his little spirit, but simply because he's normal. He: bites people, throws hairbrushes into toilet bowls, sticks marbles and buttons into his nose, swallows keys and safety pins, falls out of windows, sticks fingers into electrical outlets, hold his breath for twenty minutes while turning blue, locks himself into bathrooms, gets lost in supermarkets, finger-paints walls with iodine, disappears from his crib at night, walks out into the street naked, puts pennies between the keys of the piano, etc., etc., etc.

No mother should be ashamed to admit that the joys of motherhood start when the kids are either asleep, away, or well married. Among the great numbers of people who have volunteered to go to the moon are several thousand young mothers who have offered either themselves or their children. The height of parental maturity is, of course, to learn to live with your child as he is—even if he is just like you.

❈❈❈❈❈

In my childhood parents spoke either English or some foreign language which both parents and children understood. They described us as good kids, rotten kids, nice kids, as the situation merited. We knew where we stood and so did our parents. We have now added a language hurdle to the ordinary problems of communication between parents and children. The average mother spouts quasi-psychiatric jargon with ease. Words like neurotic, introverted, extroverted, complex, psychosomatic, escapist are part of any young parent's household vocabulary—words used more frequently than they are understood. The experts themselves hardly agree on the definitions. I recently saw a panel of psychiatrists on a program called "Getting Along with People" almost come to blows over the meaning of "well-adjusted."

I offer here a few definitions which may be helpful.

1. *High I.Q. child:* A kid who says dirty words earlier than other kids—usually a grandchild.

2. *Auto-suggestion:* The parental compulsion to jump into an auto (or in front of one) and get away from it all.

3. *Siblings:* Children of the same parents, each of whom is perfectly normal until they get together.

4. *Hallucinations:* Seeing visions of kids without running noses.

5. *Self-expression:* In a child, any act which cannot be explained rationally.

6. *Subconscious:* Seething, fuming, foaming, raging, suppressed feelings deep inside struggling for release. (In the old days they called them gas pains.)

7. *Sex Maniac:* A husband who wants more children.

❁❁❁❁❁

It doesn't take long for a child to learn how to play the psychology game, not so much with his mother as against her. Playing with mental blocks is a game at which two can play, and the kid can win hands down, since he has caught onto the fact that punishment of the child is at the top of the tabu list. He, however, can punish his mother with impunity. The apprentice tries out his skill on his master:

MOTHER: "I will not buy you that paint set."
CHILD: "If you don't I may get hostile and vomit."

MOTHER: "I will not buy you that bicycle."
CHILD: "You really hate me, don't you?"

MOTHER: "I'm sorry I let you have the ice cream."
CHILD: "If you are truly sorry I will forgive you."

CHILD: "Don't scream, mother. It's bad for you. Reason with me, mother. Dr. Spock wouldn't be very proud of you."

The "sympathetic" parent of today finds himself pushed around by his kids more than his "unsympathetic" parents ever did.

I have seen young tyrants turn their parents against each other. Since the mother is afraid to, or has been advised not to show anger in the presence of the child, she stores up a full day's supply of venom which she spits at her husband when he comes home. The parents blame each other, each other's parents and each other's lack of courage. Children have precipitated as many divorces as adultery and incompatibility. Many a home, like a toy, has been broken by a child with a hammer given to him by his parents.

❁❁❁❁❁

Many young mothers, driven by fear of not doing enough for their children, are imposing upon them the kind of frenetic care that converts the home into a hospital and childhood into a critical condition.

The "privileged" baby starts out in life in a room decorated in antiseptic modern, surrounded by sterilizing equipment, funnels, forceps, tweezers, jars, tongs, brushes, bandages, scales and test tubes. His first sense impressions of home will be compounded of rubbing alcohol, talcum powder, ammonia, and warm milk—fortified, enriched, improved, refined, flavored, reconstituted to "resemble" mother's milk, served in a container which does not resemble, by a woman whose face is hidden behind an anonymous mask. What used to be a kitchen—a place where people would eat, drink and talk—is now a steam room. Down at the bottom of a twenty-gallon pot boiling on the stove is one bottle nipple which an unsterile (eight kids) grandma had recklessly touched.

It is just as taxing to be a child today as it is to be a mother. Statistics show an increase of ulcers and colitis in American children, a condition brought on by the undue anxiety of "educated" mothers who find their civilized environment far more menacing and potentially evil than their "ignorant" counterparts in some Pacific island who have only a witch doctor to consult. In short, the kid has to wear a sweater because his mother is chilly.

The seeds of fear implanted in the infant are potent enough to make him a full-blown hypochondriac by the age of six. "Go out and play, but don't run. You'll get perspired." Perspiration is the first symptom of the Black Plague. Today any kid can get out of doing anything by simply announcing, "But, Ma, I'll sweat." Some mothers feel that a tendency to perspire should automatically classify their sons in 4F.

There are enough child-care tabus rampant today to destroy all the fun of childhood. I have seen mothers take their little ones to the beach and keep them out of the water all day because 1. in the morning the water is too cold; 2. noon seems pretty good but it's too close to lunchtime; 3. after lunch you must not go into the water because you get cramps; besides one should rest after lunch till three o'clock, which is milk-and-cookies time, after which you cannot go into the water after eating, which brings us to about 4 P.M. when the air is too cool. When the air is warm 4. the water is cold, and nobody is in the water to keep an eye on you, and you know what happened to that little boy who didn't listen, but 5. "we can sit on the beach until six and watch the sun go into the water." I heard one kid suggest, "Ma, if I don't eat tomorrow all day may I go in swimming the day after tomorrow?"

"If you take two naps."

I have seen kid-napping mothers rush out into the street, abduct their child, and force him to take an afternoon nap in a crib he outgrew four years before. This "twilight sleep" makes him an insomniac at night, a condition that calls for tranquilizers.

From dawn till dark the mother's voice announces the imminence of danger:

"Don't touch that lollipop; it's got germs. Richard touched it. Richard had a cold last winter. You don't want to catch his cold, do you?"

"Stand back from the TV set. Don't you see the announcer has a stuffed nose?"

"Don't forget to take off your glasses when you're not looking at anything."

The fellow who claims that kids today have "too much

freedom" hasn't been watching carefully. When the mother takes the baby out for a stroll in his carriage he is strapped around the waist, under the armpits, over the shoulders, and into a crash helmet buckled under his chin. If the carriage went off a cliff this kid wouldn't get a scratch.

In his high chair (modeled after the electric chair) his feet are pinned down, there are two belts crisscrossing his chest, and his hands are manacled to prevent him from doing violence to himself.

His playpen is a solitary-confinement padded cell in which he is tethered by ropes with bells on them to warn of a possible break. Built into one wall is an abacus on which the prisoner can count off the days of his sentence. Food is placed in the pen in an unbreakable cup which he bangs against the bars to get attention. Since he has not yet learned to talk we must assume that his "Yah, yah" means what it usually does in prison movies: "I'm not eating this slop. Get me a lawyer."

When they send him out for fresh air they seal him into an upholstered Eskimo suit, lower him into fisherman's boots and tie a scarf in a strangulation knot around his neck. It takes about an hour and a half to get the contemporary child dressed to go out and play for eight minutes.

⊗⊗⊗⊗⊗

Many young mothers take crash courses for early admission to mental institutions. They meet at the check-out counter of the local supermarket every afternoon for seminars. While the babies are sitting in the shopping carts breaking open cereal boxes the mothers are at work breaking down each other's nervous systems:

"Does yours suck his thumb? Tsk! Tsk! It's a diverted sex urge, you know. Better he should wet his bed."

"Mine doesn't wet his bed."

"It's better that he should than suppress it and suck his thumb."

"Maybe he feels unwanted. His thumb is probably a father symbol."

"Does yours walk yet? No? And he's eleven months old? Maybe he's got soft bones. Maybe he doesn't want to walk. Maybe he's too weak."

"I feed mine on the scale to see how well he is gaining."

"I keep mine in bed until his temperature goes down to ninety-six point seven."

"I never let my mother near mine. She kisses him."

"I never wrap his feet in his blanket. It stops him from growing."

"I buy mine shoes two sizes too large so his feet will grow."

"Mine cries at night."

"I get up at night to see why he isn't crying."

"I would like to have another baby but my apartment is too small."

"How soon do they get 'dry'?"

"It's just pot luck, I say."

The mother is afraid to wait too long to start training him, but how long is too long? She is also afraid of too soon. How soon is too soon? Too early training, she has heard, can make a child a slow reader. At any rate she would like him to keep up with his "peers." She has tried "anticipating"—watching for that especially angelic expression that comes over a child's face just before. If he suddenly stands still, that too is a pretty good sign.

The road to dryness is strewn with the bodies of young mothers whose nervous systems could not take the shock of the sudden changes from wet to dry and back again ("He was completely trained when he suddenly untrained himself"); who could not believe that a normal child would do it *next* to the potty; or as soon as he got *off* the potty; or lead his mother to a dark corner under the staircase and point with pride ("I made a poopoo") to what he could have done just as easily *on* the potty. The mother begins to suspect that he is withholding deliberately, that the little accidents are not accidents at all; that he is using the potty to reward or punish her.

It seems to this mother that her child likes to do everything in the bathroom except use the potty. He likes to play there, eat there, float boats there, play games with the rolls of paper, wrapping himself up like a mummy, even take baths there—but he resists going to pot like a man. She has nightmares in which she sees him at his wedding walking down the aisle with his wet diaper dragging on the floor.

⊗⊗⊗⊗⊗

When the little boy in school sang, "Land where my fathers died; Land of the pills inside," he knew what he was talking about. Along with salt, pepper, sugar, and ketchup, the dining-room table now displays a variety of bottles of vitamins labeled alphabetically A, B, B1, B2, B12, C, D, and in combinations like DC6, BAD, DAB, CAD, DAD, 2B or not 2B. Each pill has its own destination in the body. Some go to the eyes, some to the liver, some to the bones, others have several stops to make, and still others are just there to direct traffic. One misdirected pill can give a kid rosy feet. If one thousand units is good for the child, two thousand should be even better, and twenty-five thousand should produce as much power as a small atomic-energy plant. It won't be long before our overdosed children will have to be registered with the government.

We have vitamin-enriched our children to the point where we have finally achieved sons to look up to. They are taller than either parent or the combined height of both. This has cut corporal punishment down to near zero. Even if a parent wants to hit his son he can't reach him. One mother took her child to the doctor because he was twelve years old and six feet tall. She was told not to worry—"He'll outgrow it." For the first time in the history of the human family the fathers now get their sons' hand-me-down sports jackets.

It must be the vitamins, too, which have produced a generation of children with immense front teeth. The children's sandbox in the park resembles a trayful of bunny rabbits. Vitamins have made the teeth strong, and thumb sucking has made them crooked. Aside from the fact that thumb sucking will ruin the kid's bite (which is already worse than his bark), it has also been widely publicized as an expression of emotional insecurity. This, of course, is a reflection on the mother who cannot explain why her child who has everything she never had should be insecure. One little girl, observing her mother's great distress over her thumb sucking, offered a tranquilizing suggestion: "Suck *your* thumb, Mommy."

Thumb sucking, however, does not disturb the orthodontists, who are having a field day straightening out the tusks of kids whose X-rays reveal more teeth than they need. The orthodontist has to create lebensraum for all these exuberant teeth crawling all over each other. Some kind of order can be restored for a fee of one thousand dollars. For several years these children will eat through miniature barbed-wire fences, talk through rubber bands, and turn out looking not like either parent, but like each other.

As children grow stronger, the pediatricians grow weaker. The demands of the mothers are far greater than the needs of the children. Between an office full of healthy children (up to the age of nineteen) who are brought in once a month for their five-hundred-mile checkup by their sick mothers and the constant ringing of the phone, a successful pediatrician can cram a lifetime of practice into about ten years and retire on early disability. One pediatrician picked up the telephone at his bedside at 1 A.M. to hear: "The reason I called you so late at night, Doctor, is because I don't like to bother you in the daytime when you're so busy."

If he has a sense of humor, he can extend his life by about three years. The successful pediatrician can dismiss silly calls with a quip because he knows that once he has been labeled "wonderful" (the equivalent of a graduate degree) by the neighborhood Women's Corps, he is "in" for keeps. As long as he says the kid is bright for his age and calls the mothers "darling," he will remain the Albert Schweitzer of the baby jungle.

"Doctor, he's not getting any heavier."

"Try carrying him for one block, darling."

"But, Doctor, this is my first baby. I don't even know where to begin."

"Keep one end full and the other dry, darling."

"Doctor, the baby isn't sleeping."

"Put his ear to the phone and I'll sing him a lullaby, darling."

"Doctor, he ate a handful of sand."

"Give him lots of water, and see that he doesn't swallow any cement, darling."

An article on child care in a popular magazine like *Readers' Digest* will trigger a barrage of phone calls from mothers.

"Doctor, the article says that breast feeding is superior to bottle feeding."

"Try one of each and let me know."

As any good pediatrican will tell you, it is these vitamin-complexed mothers who browbeat their doctors into giving shots where they do absolutely no good. Any pediatrician who refuses to punch the kid full of miracle drugs will lose his practice. So, he becomes a "pusher," knowing full well that the reaction to the wonder drugs is sometimes worse than the disease. By the time the child is four years old his rear end looks like a dart board. I often wonder whether some anthropologist has studied the possible relationship between sticking needles into kids' fannies and sticking pins into voodoo dolls to ward off evil spirits.

The kids today will never know how soft we had it. We could stay out of school for a week with an ordinary running nose and get huge quantities of tea and sympathy. Today the child is cured in twenty-four hours and finds himself back in school scrounging around for a forty-eight- or seventy-two-hour virus.

&&&&&

Just when the parent thinks he has it made, when all the inoculations have been given, and the chicken pox and measles and mumps have come and gone without having done much damage, thank God, and the child's mind seems to be functioning normally, Junior gets the drooping jaw and stupid expression of a young Neanderthal man. You are ashamed to admit that this erstwhile intelligent child who now can just about manage "Dib be a peddy, Daddy" is your son. You keep him home so the outside world won't know and you brace yourself for one of the standard traumatic experiences of family life—the kid's tonsil operation. And while you're at it, get those adenoids, too, for they are co-conspirators in this plot to cut off the oxygen supply to your child's brain.

The parents decide to have the tonsils out, but the doctors (as usual) don't quite agree. There is the "Don't take them out; nature put them there for a reason" school vs. the "Take them out; they only make trouble" school. There are also the "It's not urgent" vs. "Don't wait" schools, as well as the winter vs. summer schools. Also the

"If he has a cold it's better to wait" vs. "It doesn't matter if he has a cold" schools. (Waiting till he gets over his cold may take several winters.)

While the parents are in the living room trying to make a decision the vaporizer is going in the bedroom and the child is lying there in the fine mist fondling his trachea and mumbling "Whadyusay, Baba?"

Now we need the opinion of a specialist. For twenty-five dollars you get the answer that will put an end to this unbearable indecision. You will hear the soft but comforting voice of authority, which will say, "It's up to you."

This calls for an act of heroism on the part of the parent. A date on the calendar is circled in red as T day. Of course, there must be some preoperative preparation. The wrong approach to childhood surgery may cause many neuroses later in life. How do you prepare the child? "Look, kid. We all had our tonsils out. Me, Uncle Al, Ed Sullivan, Arthur Godfrey, Stephen, Eric . . ."

"I don't like Stephen and I'm not going."

The psychologists say, "Tell him it will hurt." That will leave you with only one problem—how to get him out of the closet to complete the psychological conditioning. Some people (not psychologists) say that the best time to tell him it will hurt is after he comes out of the ether, when he is too weak to kick you.

It is wise, some suggest, for the child to get used to the sight of blood. Let him play with the ketchup bottle, or watch medic shows on TV. We got our boy a Little Doctor's Play Kit containing knives, syringes, hypodermic needles, stethoscope, head mirror, tongue depressors and thermometer. (My brother Joe opened his first office with less than this.) We had to stop our precocious surgeon from performing an illegal operation on his salamander.

By this time the child is beginning to feel you are ready to make him an offer for the surrender of his tonsils. "Say, Dad, how about if I go for the tonsils operation you maybe will buy me a seventy-two-foot Erector set, and a hundred-and-twelve-inch TV screen?" Agreed.

We're now ready. The pretonsilectomy primer says: "The doctor should personally escort the child into the operating room." You remember from a composition you wrote in the eighth grade that "escort" means "a body of armed guards attending another for his protection." You are not sure, but you are not going to ask whether for a public execution of this type he is entitled to a minister, two men from the press, two state troopers and two witnesses.

As they wheel the boy into the operating room you wave goodbye calmly, knowing that you have prepared him psychologically, emotionally, and physically. You have behaved like an intelligent, responsible father. You have done right by your child. It shows in the expression on the little boy's face, an expression that says, "You traitor, my own father selling his flesh and blood for a bowl of vanilla ice cream. If I ever come back I'm gonna get you for this!"

And he does come back, and he does get you, during the period known as convalescence. "Read to me. Ice cream. Sing to me. Ice cream. Blow my nose. Ice cream. Cover my feet. Play cards with me. Stand on your head. Change the channel. Where's that Erector set?" followed very soon by the revolt of the parent, who, once he is sure the child will survive, comes back with: "Blow your own nose. So it's not a hundred-and-twelve-inch screen; so it's a seven-inch screen. Get going, pal. Maybe you forgot how to walk!"

After four months of preparation, and a week of post-operative living with blood, sweat, and tears, all you want to know is: Why does he still look stupid, why does he still catch colds, why does he still talk through his nose, and why has he given up saying "Dib be a peddy, Daddy," and now says "Dib be a dibe, Daddy"?

You go back to the doctor who said "Take them out." He now says "It may be psychosomatic. It comes from the mind." Do you now have to wait till his mind dries up before his nose dries up? The kid is back again under his vaporizer rainbow asking, "Wod do we do dow, Daddy?"

Another doctor says, "It may be an allergy." If he has an allergy one thing is certain—he is allergic. To what? How do we find out? By playing a counting-out game called Running Nose Roulette. Maybe it's his pillow. Out, pillow, out! The first three nights his nose runs because he is crying for his pillow, so you can't tell yet. Run, nose, run.

Maybe it's his mattress. Out, mattress, out. Here's a kid who can afford the best. He is now sleeping on a board without a pillow, like a hermit. Run, nose, run. You remove the blankets. Now you can't tell whether his nose is running because he is cold or because he's allergic. Run, nose, run.

Everything in his bed is canceled out as negative. Maybe it's some "foreign body" in the room—either the dog or Grandma. Both are banished to the cellar until the experiments are completed. Run, nose, run.

Maybe it's the sunshine. Aha! The shades are drawn. The kid's nose is now running from bumping it against the furniture in the dark.

Dust is next on the list. The rugs, curtains, and window shades are removed. The rumor gets around the neighborhood that your family is moving. Passers-by come in to inquire about the apartment.

You get no results on your own so you go to an allergy specialist. He tells you as he blows his nose that there is very little in the world that does not bring tears to the eyes of some sensitive soul somewhere—moustache wax, white whale oil, condor feathers, Tibetan monastery incense, Santa Claus reindeers, Stradivarius violins, twelfth-century illuminated manuscripts. Some people are even allergic to allergists. Nothing can be dismissed as insignificant until all the tests have been made. The victim is punched so full of holes, his nose is now running from the draft.

The allergist finally sends the family his report: "We don't know exactly what he is allergic to, but we have definitely ascertained that he is not allergic to, and can have as much as he wants of, bark of trees, ground glass, plaster, untanned leather, unfinished bronze, bubble gum, dehydrated water, dry ice and arsenic."

Baby's bedtime is the twilight zone of sanity in the child-centered home. The child has strengthened himself for the ordeal by taking a short nap before lunch and a longer one after. Out of consideration for his daddy who has been away at work all day, the youngster has set aside the evening hours for the purpose of bringing the father up to the mother's level of nervous frustration. This time of day is known as Nightmare at Sundown. It was probably during these hours that Romulus and Remus were left on a Roman hillside.

The *danse macabre* usually begins at about 6 P.M., when the child starts to kick, bite, fall, or just run around in circles making weird, grunting noises. This wild burst of energy is usually attributed to his being "sleepy" and is the clue for the cooperative all-American lover-boy-daddy to say, "Let *me* take him to his room." The little boy, draped over the shoulder of his daddy, makes as sweet and sentimental a scene as a *Saturday Evening Post* cover. It lasts until the kid hits the pillow.

I went through all this with my own boy. He slept fine all day. We used to find him out cold under the piano, behind armchairs, on steep staircases. Often sleep would close in on him during a meal. I would pick him up, his head still in the farina, carry him to his bed, and slip him gently under his fleecy, fluffy, downy little blanket. Then it would start.

"I'm hungry."

You can't let any child of yours go to bed hungry, so you fill the crib with cookies, bananas and fruitcake. He swallows one bite of banana and squeezes the rest into a paste which he massages into his hair.

"O.K. Now our little man is not hungry any more, is he? Close your little eyes and off to dreamland."

"I'm lonesome."

Well! We know what to do, don't we? We give him the things he loves for security's sake. You fill his crib with what you, not he, call his "widdle sweddie," his "skatesies," his "trainsy-set," his "teddsy bearsies . . ."

"Now we're not lonesome any more, are we? Just close your eyes and you'll see a moving picture."

"I saw it last night. Anyhow, I'm afraid to stay here by myself."

"What are you afraid of?"

"There's a bear in the closet."

No use trying to dissuade him. If he says there's a bear in the closet, agree with him. Go into that closet and face the beast like a man. I did it, more than once. I struggled with my wife's fur piece, kicked up quite a fuss, came out in a cold sweat and announced triumphantly, "He's dead. Go to sleep."

"You forgot to kiss me good night."

I kiss him good night. "No good," he says. "You kissed me, but I didn't kiss you." Take two! We do it over till we can synchronize our kisses and "make the scene."

"I didn't say good night to Grandma."

Grandma is subpoenaed. She still goes in for crib-rocking in a big way—except that this crib is not a rocking crib. After Grandma has shaken loose half the nuts and bolts of the crib and the kid, she gives you that "See? You have to know how" look, takes you by the arm and you leave the room together, only to be summoned back by "Uh! uh! You didn't read to me."

Every parent has been through the reading ordeal. It left me with chronic laryngitis, a distaste for fairy tales in general and "Red Riding Hood" in particular. It was his favorite story for years. He had it memorized but insisted I read it over and over and over. If I skipped a word, "Just for that you have to start from the beginning." I came to root for the wolf, hoping that some day the hunter wouldn't make it in time.

The bloodthirsty wolf makes him thirsty.

"I'm thirsty," says my young insomniac.

"O.K. Fill her up!" I let him have all he can take—pitchers full. "Drink up! Happy New Year!"

"Now I gotta go weewee."

You can't rush these things. Under pressure it takes longer than usual to start things going. There is lots of flushing, but not much going—at least not for the kid. He has everyone in the house going but himself.

The kid may not be sleepy, but he's no fool, either. When he sees the arteries in his father's fist begin to quiver he quickly becomes a "good boy," and disarms you with a cooing "Good night, Daddy. I love you," entwining his little arms about your windpipe, bringing on that choked-up feeling.

"Good night, sweet prince." It was worth it. All your suspicions that he was giving you the works were obviously unfounded. He is now lying in his crib looking like a Bellini angel. As you make your way back to the kitchen to finish your cold coffee, there's a scream from the bedroom.

"Daddy! I —"

Now you've had it. The last button of sanity has just popped. This is justifiable bratricide. No male jury will convict you.

"This is the last time I'm gonna tell you for the last time. If I have to go up there one more time I'm gonna murder you!"

"O.K., Daddy. When you come up to murder me bring up a glass of water."

Then I discovered that when he finally ran out of ideas

he would suck his thumb until he fell asleep. When all other methods failed I would thumb my nose at the rule book and simply shove his thumb into his mouth. Out cold in three minutes. For a while I entertained the idea of putting on the market a plastic nursing bottle in the shape of a thumb.

8888888

There are ironies in this tug of war as profound as they are pathetic. The child, unaware of his "need for his own room," is trying to work his way to where other people are. Alone can sometimes be lonely. His instinctive craving for the nest is drawing him back to the kitchen. He wants to hear familiar (in the pure sense of family) voices, see familiar faces and smell familiar food. But we want to do "more" for him than our parents did for us. One of the side effects of "Operation More" is often "Separation More."

I saw something frightening in a medical journal—a picture of a child sleeping with its hand resting on a bosom-shaped object. Under the picture were these words: "Nipponese Nap Inducer—Latest device for soothing infants is Japanese device known as mother heart. The device contains a mechanism that produces the rhythm and sound of a woman's heart for an hour after being charged from an electrical outlet." Mother love, AC-DC.

8888888

The great dream of our poor parents was for higher education for their children. The middle-class mother today announces that her two-year-old will go to college.

"My problem," she says, "is how to get him out of the house *now*."

The richer the family, the better it can afford this separatism. Kids who come from the "best" homes, those in which books, records and painting sets are plentiful, are the first to receive the benefits of subsidized apartheid at nursery school. The mother's lack of faith in herself as teacher, and in her home as a good enough environment for her child, added to her understandable desire for a few child-free hours per day, have her out nursery-school shopping long before the child is housebroken. There are long waiting lists for the "better" schools. Some children do not get in before they are thirteen years old. "Better," in schools as in bicycles, means more expensive, and "best" means most expensive. There are also pre-nursery, and even pre-haps schools. The latter are the Ivy League group to which one must "commit" the child as soon as the mother suspects she is pregnant.

There are nursery schools which are truly educational institutions. They understand children, love them, and seek to recognize and foster creativity. Too many nursery schools, unfortunately, provide little more than group baby-sitting and amusement, a service for which many mothers pay a high fee just to get their kids off their hands. Early each morning these kids are left outside their homes alongside the garbage cans to be picked up by the lorries of such institutions as Peter-Pumpkin-on-the-Hudson, Humpty-Dumpty-on-the-Rocks, or Pied Piper Pre-prep.

The tuition for the more select ("private"—a word which many parents erroneously define as "superior") schools is about the same as for medical school. In order not to appear discriminatory some schools offer scholarships to three-year-olds who are willing to wait on tables.

It is considered best to enroll the child in the spring. Winter sessions have a limited course of study, since the faculty spends all morning yanking off the student body's snowsuits and all afternoon yanking them back on.

These institutions of lower learning are a training ground for living in a democracy. Children are not ordered to do things; they are consulted. Would we like to paint, rest, listen, clap hands?

"Shall we all go to the bathroom?"

"Let's take a vote."

If the majority decides to put off going to the bathroom, the one who has to go must learn to live in a democracy. The chronic wetters are handled by appealing to their group loyalty as well as their personal pride. The teacher gives out gold stars for a clear day and gray stars for a cloudy day. There is an honor society for kids who can zip their own pants.

Here, too, the child can develop skills that he could not possibly pick up at home, such as cutting paper with dull scissors, pipe-cleaner sculpture, linoleum cutting (if he tried this at home he'd get his head handed to him), and sitting on the floor in a circle even when he is alone.

The dance is required for all. (Some of the children from the suburbs, however, have to be taught to walk before they are ready for the dance. Between school buses and family cars they have never found out about ambulation.) The Falling Leaves ballet is very popular, as is the Opening Bud. I witnessed a spectacular Ice Cream Cone ballet in which the children were expressing the feeling of melting in three flavors (individual differences) . Awkward children are given remedial skipping.

In another room, that same day, a group of boys was being urged to feel like airplanes, directed by the teacher-pilot in the control tower.

"Richard, where would you like to fly?"

"I would like to fly to Japan."

"Good."

"And Marvin, where would you like to fly?"

"I would like to fly to China."

"Good."

"And Arthur, where would you like to fly?"

"I would like to fly home."

Not so good. This kind of self-expression is discouraged.

In some of the more elegant schools they teach French. One father told me that the reason he sent his little boy to one of these finishing schools for the hardly begun was to rid him of the vulgar habit of saying "Hey, pa; hey, ma." It worked. After only three months he was saying "Hey, père; hey, mère." The kid reported to his father that one unfinished boy at his école had for some reason called him a "little basket" in English.

Much of the curriculum is planned to direct the latent or overt hostility of children toward each other into proper channels. Some children are chronic hitters. Others are chronic nonhitters. To hit or not to hit, that is the question. The psychologists are concerned with both types. The hitters should be discouraged from hitting, and the nonhitters should be encouraged to hit, since it is better to hit than to harbor hostility.

Peaceful coexistence can be as strenuous for a child as for an adult. My little girl, Emily, came home from school

one day in a state of near exhaustion: "All day long
sharing, sharing, sharing." When Emily brought home a
bump on her head I asked her what happened. "It happened during the rest period," she explained. "I was resting better than anybody in the whole class, but Georgie
was restless."

The teacher in the role of peacemaker finds herself
face to face with some precocious rationalizations for
violence at the preschool level:

"Why did you hit Gregory?"
"Because he hit me back first."

"If you hit Freddie you will hurt him and he will have
to go to the doctor."
"He should go anyhow. He's got a running nose."

"Georgie wanted to hit me."
"How do you know that he wanted to hit you?"
"He hit me, so I guess he wanted to."

Even subtler are the ways in which these little ones
have learned to defeat the enemy through psychological
warfare:

"Alice and I are going to play house today, Evelyn. You
can play too. You can be the maid and this is your day off."

Two kids plunked themselves down on the same little
fire engine at the same time. The seasoned strategist said,
"One at a time could have more fun, Robert—if you got
off."

It comes as a great shock to many parents when they
discover that the child's definition of "opportunity" does

not always harmonize with their own. One parent went to pick up his child after nursery school. He was greeted with "Daddy, I was made a helper today, and the teacher sent me to pick up the toys that were left on the sidewalk outside the building. You know something, Daddy? I could have escaped!"

❦❦❦❦❦

Some five million American children now go (or are sent) to summer camp. The vast majority of the campers come not from the tenements but from nice middle-class, sunny homes that already provide grass and fresh air. Nothing looks more like a deserted village than a beautiful suburban community in the summertime. This mass migration of well-to-do children to child sanctuaries each July 1st is another manifestation of the Separatist Movement. There are good camps for children, camps that do bring to a city child an understanding of the nature of nature, that let the physically and aesthetically indoor child out of his cage to fly about in the great outdoors with other birds of this feather who flock together. Most middle-class parents, however, select a camp for their children by such educational criteria as who goes there and the number of foam-rubber mattresses per child.

The only experience our family ever had with summer camping happened this way. When my brother Albert was about eight he was selected from a group of poor neighborhood kids because he looked, as Mama said, "greener and yellower" than all the rest, to be sent to a farm in upstate New York for a month to see if some red and pink could be added to the yellow and green. After about two weeks Papa went up to see how Albert was doing. When we met the train the next night it was not Papa but Albert who stepped onto the platform.

"Albert! Where's Papa?"

"In the country. He said he needs the vacation more than I do, so he took the last two weeks."

There is a legend that tells how middle-class camping (roughing it royally) came into existence. Once upon a time there were a king and queen who lived in a large castle and had all they could ask of the good things in life. Deep in their hearts, though, they were unhappy about their young son, Prince Blasé the Great, who was driving his parents to king-size distraction. "There's nothing to do around here" was his constant refrain.

He wandered about the castle aimlessly, skin-dived in the mossy moat, gave hotfoots to the guards in armor, played with torches or with his Little Merlin Magic Kit, smeared up the walls of the vast dining hall with his little mosaic set, and stayed up late yocking at the stale gags of the court jester.

The king and queen, realizing they had a behavior problem on their hands, consulted Zip, the chief sorcerer, and came to a decision: "We've got to get the princeling out of the castle!" They called in the leader of the gypsy band that lived in the nearby forest and made him an offer: "Take the prince into your band for a few months, teach him the lore of the forest, to hunt and to fish and to know the songs of the birds and the language of the beasts, and instruct him in the crafts of your people. For this we shall reward you amply." The leader of the band agreed to the terms, and this is how the first kid went off to a private summer camp.

With minor variations the practice still exists.

Our neighbors were signing the necessary documents for sending their boy off to camp for the first time, in the presence of the camp owner and two counselors. Watching all this was the younger brother. After a respectful silence of about five minutes, he looked up with tears in his eyes and asked his father, "Why are we selling Robert?"

The richer the kid, the more "incidentals" he will have to take to camp: four pairs of short shorts, four pairs of long shorts, four pairs of medium-short longs, warm, medium, and cool pajamas with long, medium, and short sleeves, spiked shoes, spikeless shoes, T shirts with V necks, sneakers for tennis and sneakers not for tennis, house slippers, warm socks, cold socks, red socks, blue socks, baseball socks, tennis socks, a laundered bag for dirty laundry, a drizzle coat, a raincoat, and an ax. There is one consolation in all this. He will come home with most of the same items (sometimes even more than he took), but none of them will be his own. Some camps do not require any of these things. In fact, if you send the money you can keep the kid at home all summer. No matter how much equipment the child takes along, about one week after he gets to camp the parents will start receiving the "send-me" post cards: "Dear Mom: Send me a compass, a canoe, a camera, a fish tank, a road map of Alaska . . ."

The kid has been instructed by his family to write every day, so he does:

DEAR MOM:
Last night a mad hermit killed all the kids.
Your late son, ERIC.

This letter, of course, was a pure fabrication. It's been raining for eight days and he has gone stir-crazy.

One of the advantages of going to summer camp (rich or poor) is that the child is introduced to a new way of life. Kids in camp are no longer just a bunch of kids. They are divided by the administration into Indian tribes, insect colonies, or animal groups: Seminoles, Iroquois, Comanches, Shawnees, Cherokees (each tribe has its chief—Sleeping Counselor), or Bumblebees, Hornets, Reindeers, Wolves, Lions, and Cobras. There are Indian tribal rites, incantations, sacrifices, mystical campfire ceremonies, secret signals, and native arts. (There are camps obliging enough to provide ready-made Indian wallets for kids who would rather go swimming than go Indian.)

We have heard of camps which are callously indifferent to the plight of the Indian. They stress photography (this requires that the boy spend most of the summer in the darkroom); nature study, which includes identification of snakes (friendly and unfriendly), birds (friendly and un-friendly), fish (friendly and unfriendly), minerals (friendly and unfriendly), mushrooms (friendly and un-friendly; handicrafts (beating an unfriendly copper plate into earrings); music and dramatics (involving every last child—if only as part of a group of "passing strangers").

No matter what a kid majors in, campfires are required for all. This brings all the kids together in close contact with each other and with the mosquitoes. By the end of the summer even the mosquitoes can hum "Old Mac-Donald Had a Farm."

Camp life builds a well-rounded individual. A kid develops imagination: ("I cannot tell a lie. Louie wet my bed") ;

initiative: ("Let's sneak over to the girls' camp"); resourcefulness: ("Let's pretend we're dead"); leadership: ("Hey, gang, let's ask for our money back").

When the camper comes home in the fall, he is generally a "new boy"—more courteous, more manly, better able to get along with others. This lasts for about three weeks, after which he becomes his normal self again, except that he has acquired new hobbies. The mother should not be shocked to find him sleeping with a snake, starting a smudge fire next to his bed to kill the mosquitoes, or leaving his room via a rope hanging from the window.

I think the time is ripe for a children's camp for parents. I feel that those of us who never went to camp would really appreciate it. Think of what we parents might learn at camp: how to get along with each other, to share things. We might have our meals served to us, our beds made for us, get eight hours of sound sleep, and have our kids send *us* money every week, which we could keep in wallets we made with our own hands.

It might also be very enlightening to invite a group of country kids to spend the summer in Manhattan, where they could learn the folkways of the metropolis. We could arrange a program of long hikes on hot pavements, subway trips during the rush hour to see nature (human) in the raw, street games in traffic, soot-breathing contests, and meeting street gangs (friendly and unfriendly).

When parents begin to feel guilty about this separatism for the "good" of their children, a deliberate attempt is made to balance the budget of love by setting aside clearly designated and carefully programed hours of "fun to-gether." This is supposed to eradicate any feelings of deser-tion which the child may have developed during his periods of exile.

The quantity of time spent is equated with the quality.

I was raised in an atmosphere of unscheduled love. Like punishment, it appeared wherever and whenever the situa-tion called for it—during, between, after, or before. It was woven into the fabric of our daily life. It was never announced; it was felt. It was certainly not the amount of time our fathers spent with us that made us feel loved. Most of them worked so hard and long we did not get to see very much of them. We regarded their hard work in the sweatshops, however, as ample proof of their devotion.

Children are more often embarrassed by pal-parents than inspired by them. My father did not fear that I might think less of him because he didn't join me in my games. If I said to my father, "Its a great day for the park," he would reply, "You're right. Go!" If I said I had no one to play with, he countered with, "So don't play." As a working man his rest was precious to him, and we were taught to respect it.

Now we are in the era of love by appointment. "Up, up everybody. This is the day. Look happy, or I'll clout you. How about a little calisthenics? Throw me the ball and I'll throw it back to you while Mommy snaps the picture for our Fun Album." The father tries to make good as social director of a quick cruise through Hand-in-Hand Land. Off to the zoos, parks, rides. March! Hep 2, 3, 4! Hep 2, 3, 4! The kids see through the entire charade but go along because they love their daddy and don't want to hurt his feelings. After all, it's only for a few hours.

Someone has suggested the formation of an organization to be called Palcoholics Anonymous, to protect weak heads of families. When the temptation becomes too great, a father can dial SHNOOK 8–1000, and two men will come and remove him to some safe place. The sponsor of this organization was a father who, before he realized how far he had strayed into palcoholism, found himself driving his kid around for Trick or Treat.

❈❈❈❈❈

The fear of "depriving" our children has produced the most "gifted" generation of children in our history. We shower them with gifts to prove our love, with the inevitable result that the gift of love has degenerated into a love of gifts.

Are we offering things as parent substitutes? Are we offering presents in place of presence? Are we giving things because we are reluctant to give time, or self, or heart? Are we bribing our children, making deals, buying their affection? ("All a kid needs are love and securities.") Are we asking them to accept tokens of our love in lieu of the real thing? Like Pavlov's dog, the child has become conditioned to respond to the ringing of the doorbell with visions of goodies. "Whadija bring me?" We have developed the strange phenomenon of the "expectant child," for whom the present is not an event to be remembered but for whom every event calls for a present. The world owes him a giving. We have reached the point in our lives where the salesman no longer asks "What does he need?" but "What doesn't he have?"

Once the habit of receiving is established, "withdrawal"

becomes difficult. The child has become a toy addict. He no longer asks "Whom shall I play with?" but "What shall I play with?" With time he needs larger doses of toys, and the parents, unwilling to watch his suffering, will provide. To deny him at this point would be too painful. It now takes sixteen toys to provide a "kick."

The more toys he has, the less he plays. He spends more time choosing than playing. He is suffering from the boredom of opulence. For the mother this abundance ultimately creates a housing problem. There is danger of fallout from every closet.

Not all toys that are labeled "educational" are. What the child needs is a simple toy—one that will call upon his imagination, his creative abilities, his time, his thought, his hands, his affection, his participation. What he is offered more and more of these days are the dehumanized, mechanized, battery-operated, remote-controlled toys that leave the child with nothing to do but watch.

Goodbye forever to the maternal affection little girls bestowed upon rag dolls, those wonderful practice babies who were hugged to pieces, dragged about in shoe boxes, slept with, sung to and loved. In the child's imagination that rag doll talked, sang, cried. The mechanized doll of today does not need anyone's sense of fantasy in order to come alive. It does, in fact, sing, wink, drink, talk, wet, gag, hiccup, recite, swallow safety pins and develop diaper rash. Sometimes the wires cross and instead of singing it wets. In many instances it walks better than its owner. The time will come when this overprivileged little doll, like its owner, is going to come up with a prerecorded "There's nothing to do around here."

A Danish architect, C.T. Sorensen, started a revolution

in Copenhagen not long ago when he designed a playground and filled it with the kind of toys for children that they cannot resist: scrap metal, pieces of lumber, corrugated boxes, wooden crates, old tree trunks, large sections of sewer pipe, and just plain junk. This is a noble attempt to give privileged kids some of the advantages I had.

❋❋❋❋❋

Just as Mama had to wage a constant battle against her environment, my wife and I, once we had moved into the middle class, found ourselves trying to keep the "better" environment from undermining our children. With success came the golden opportunity to give our children *everything*. We were never quite sure at what point we were giving them more than was good for them. We wondered whether giving them goods equaled doing them good, whether it might not be better to hold back and give them only *some* of the good things in life rather than *all*, whether the experience of achieving success was not a greater gift than prepackaged success, whether we were not handing out unachieved rewards. We came to realize, too, that the founding fathers were wise, indeed, in guaranteeing only the *pursuit* of happiness. They knew that happiness cannot be conferred or guaranteed.

We have two fine children who reflect my wife's (more than my own) ability to pull in the reins when we found ourselves giving them what we could *afford* rather than what they *needed*.

It has become increasingly difficult to distinguish between necessities and luxuries in a world in which the
unnecessary is touted day and night as necessary. The
merchandisers have done the job of creating appetites so
well that we seem to *need* everything. It is almost un-
patriotic to say "I don't want it even if I can afford it."
The Bible says "Thou shalt not covet," but the hawkers
say "Thou shalt."

We wondered, along with many other middle-class parents, whether we were doing the right thing in removing
all the discomforts we had experienced, whether making
it unnecessary for the middle-class child to walk, wait,
worry, work, perspire, or cry was good for him.

A disadvantage may turn out to have been an advantage,
a denial an incentive, a deprivation an inspiration. Running interference for the child so that he will never get
hurt may maim him for life. There are many young men
and women today telling their psychiatrists, "My parents
did too much for me." Unearned satisfaction of one's
needs may leave a young person with a feeling of great
emptiness. Discontentment is a springboard for achievement. Life consists of tensions and relaxations. Permanent
relaxation is death.

We even wondered whether it was possible for a child,
or even an adult, to understand good without bad, abundance without scarcity, rich without poor. It is ridiculous,
of course, to say to a middle-class child, "Be poor! Go
swimming in the East River like I did." Besides, the parent
would have to drive him there and also carry all his underwater paraphernalia.

Overcompensating for one's childhood insufficiencies

has in many instances produced what the middle-class parent never anticipated—the bored child. Boredom was not one of my childhood's disadvantages; it is predominantly a middle- and upper-class syndrome. Diminishing returns in joy, the decline of enthusiasm, and the overabundance of time are painful to behold. The greatest shock of all is their unexpected envy of our "deprived" existence. "Steak again? Why can't I have a salami sandwich, like your mother used to give you?" "Take me for a ride in the subway, Daddy." "Is this where you lived, Daddy? I wish I could have lived here. You must have had a ball." Then the pendulum swings the other way. If Daddy points out that he did not have all the advantages his children have, they get annoyed and respond in chorus: "Oh, no. Here we go again!" They feel we are looking for sympathy.

It gets worse. When middle-class children are reminded by their *nouveau*-liberated parents of how good they have it, the kids come up with the equivalent of: "What are you knocking yourself out for? Do me a favor; don't do me no favors. I didn't ask you to sacrifice for me." And finally, the *coup de grâce:* "Why didn't you have more children?" This was supposed to have been the greatest advantage of all—a small family!

Now that my own children are growing up and seem to be surviving our excesses of generosity, I see that their real need is a life made by themselves rather than custom tailored by us. They want rose-colored dreams rather than color TV. They have defined the poverty of their lives in their own terms. They want to overcome. Middle-class kids in great numbers have now taken on the responsibility of fulfilling the needs of the contemporary "huddled masses yearning to breathe free." By doing this they also fulfill themselves. Now, perhaps, they will come to understand us, their parents. Separated no more.

III
Off My Chest

I should like to revert to an ancient tradition of my people which required a father to leave to his children, in addition to some earthly goods, an ethical will, the purpose of which was to transmit a summation of personal values, some articles of faith which the child, while not morally bound to accept, is urged to consider.

⁂⁂⁂⁂⁂

I believe that each newborn child arrives on earth with a message to deliver to mankind. Clenched in his little fist is some particle of yet unrevealed truth, some missing clue, which may solve the enigma of man's destiny. He has a limited amount of time to fulfill his mission and he will never get a second chance—nor will we. He may be our last hope. He must be treated as top sacred.

In a cosmos in which all things appear to have a meaning, what is *his* meaning? We who are older and presumably wiser must find the key to unlock the secret he carries within himself. The lock cannot be forced. Our mission is to exercise the kind of loving care which will prompt the child to open his fist and offer up his truth, his individuality, the irreducible atom of his self. We must provide the kind of environment in which the child will joyfully deliver his message through complete self-fulfillment.

When he is born we give him a public name. This provides only tentative identification until he finds his own true name, his potential at birth so completely realized that he and his work and his name become one. To have lived without having "made a name for himself" is virtually to have died at birth. We cannot allow him to be born a VIP and to die anonymously, often ignominiously. We cannot afford the loss of a single soul. We have already lost too many.

There are many political and social movements whose earnest purpose is to save the world. My personal commitment is to the philosophy expressed in Sanhedrin 4:5 which says that whoever destroys one life will be considered as having destroyed the whole world; and whoever saves one life will be credited with having saved the whole world.

⁂

I regard overcrowded classrooms as a major menace to individuality. It is possible to educate masses but quite impossible to teach children in masses—especially little ones. I was involved in this futile procedure as a public-school teacher. For some fifteen years I tried in vain to reconcile my "Ed" courses' philosophy of reaching the individual student with the constant presence of from thirty to forty children, some eager to stand out, just as many eager to hide out. I have seen the lifeless faces of children whose selves had never been revealed even to themselves, whose unique message will never be delivered. We should hold annual services at the grave of the Unknown Child to remind us of the millions of living children who never really come alive, whose souls remain in limbo in spite of our humanitarian declarations about the sanctity of the individual. Never to discover one's self is never to be free. The road to personal freedom goes from cognition to self-cognition, to self-recognition, to the supreme joy of recognition by others.

A "class" is an arbitrary grouping of seemingly homogeneous beings, no two of which are any more alike than two snowflakes. If it were possible to place children under a microscope, one would find the least of them inspiringly beautiful, distinctively designed. When we gather too many, flakes or children, the loveliness of individuality is lost and what we get is all white, the ultimate in neutrality.

There should be no more than fifteen children in any class. This is now being done for the "special" child. All children are special. They are not created equal. They are created different. There is hardly a child without some gift worth developing, some manifestation of his special being. All gifts are equally important. Each child's contribution to the human race is to be celebrated with much rejoicing. It is the teacher's duty to discover the seed of possibility in each child, to talent-scout the souls of little children, to insure the growth and fruition of what is best in this child, whether it is a talent for science, music, art, plumbing, or gardening—to nurture his innate ability, to help him toward self-determination through a heightened awareness of his abilities by supplying educational hearing aids to amplify the inner voice for those who cannot hear it by themselves. His voice, once identified, becomes his purpose in life; this will be the voice that will speak his message. In an overcrowded class, as in any crowd, there is a good chance that only the loud voices will be heard.

In a society which claims to value individuality we have come to place so high a premium upon conformity in children that any deviant from the "norm" is promptly pounced upon as maladjusted. This, too, is a penalty imposed upon the exceptional child because of the large class. The child who feels, talks, thinks and behaves like all the rest is "doing fine." Like the chameleon, he has learned to camouflage his identity to keep out of trouble. He presents no problem to the teacher. A good teacher should be disturbed when a child accepts everything in his environment, or even worse, becomes a hypocrite, junior grade, and feigns acceptance for fear of being declared an eccentric. The maladjusted child may be the true leader of his group. The fact that nobody follows him does not prove that he is wrong. No child should be declared maladjusted until we have given serious consideration to the possibility that *we* may be maladjusted, not he. He may be the one who is right, honest, sensitive, profound, and motivated by higher standards than the rest of us. Is it morally right to require adjustment to a society which is maladjusted? It is possible, even in a democracy, that the majority may be wrong. Inability to accept the status quo is not necessarily a sign of weakness. If the founding fathers of this country had all been well-adjusted we would still be a British colony.

We must see that each school has a staff of professional service people: social workers, psychologists and guidance counselors, who will be available full time *on the premises* (not itinerant healers) to help the teachers unravel the knots in the hearts and minds of troubled youngsters, to decode scrambled messages, to help liquidate those tensions that make children uncooperative, unreceptive and ultimately unteachable.

Big business makes sure that manpower is not lost. It provides testing bureaus, personnel experts and efficiency men to guarantee that each man will be productive. "It pays," they say. The community spends millions on mental institutions, reformatories, and the support of legions of poorly educated men and women. It still has to be convinced, however, that it pays to invest in schools that will produce personally fulfilled, socially responsible, self-disciplined human beings prepared for cooperative living in a free society.

According to the National Education Association, it costs three thousand and twenty dollars to take care of a delinquent child for nine months in an institution; for the normal child in school it costs from four hundred to eight hundred dollars.

This country abounds in college graduates who have not yet found themselves, bewildered young men and women who wander from campus to campus in search of a "major," not yet aware of the fact that the *real* major is one's self.

Too many people end up earning a living, very often an excellent one, at work they do not love, work that bears little relation to their talents, or, at best, does not "interfere" too much with their private lives. The world is full of these unhappy successfuls: doctors who should have been artists, and vice versa; dentists who should have been shoemakers, and vice versa; lawyers who should have been drummers, and vice versa. All are vocational misfits and malcontents who during their schooling were either separated from their talents or never were introduced to them. Ideally, a man should have only one regret about his work—that it ends. He should hate death primarily because it leaves his work unfinished. We are a hobby-happy country because so many men do not find joy in their work. They are split personalities living out lives not truly their own. They will never be at peace with themselves.

꒰꒱꒰꒱꒰

Once we have done everything to insure the child's recognition of his self, we have to make clear to him the relationship between his self and the selves of others. The nature of the individual's involvement with other individuals cannot be taught too early, since this involvement starts with the child's first breath and does not end until his last.

In a society which believes in education for all, the ultimate objective becomes living with all, even with those you don't like. Social justice should have nothing to do with personal likes and dislikes. The Scripture says

"Thou shalt love thy neighbor as thyself." It does not say you have to like him, nor does it say "See footnote A regarding color, shape of nose, texture of hair, ethnic classification."

The arithmetical (arithmetic + ethic) concepts of a richer personal life through gaining by sharing, multiplication of happiness by division, subtraction from the larger to add to the smaller, should be written into the day-to-day curriculum of our schools. We are now teaching ethics marginally, subliminally, incidentally—if at all. The subject of civilized human relations is too important to be left to chance.

We make much of "toughening our youth." They are tough enough. What they need is softening. Our education is heart-less. It is more important for the child's first reader to say "Love, Dick, love" than "Jump, Dick, jump." It is just as easy for a child to learn the word "pity" as it is to learn the word "kitty," "kiss" as "miss," "hug" as "bug." It is never too early to teach the shaping of emotional swords into plowshares.

A Show and Tell of kindness, even on the most elementary level, can be based upon life in the classroom.
TEACHER: "Georgie looks sad today. Let us ask him why he is sad."
ANY CHILD: "Why are you sad, Georgie?"
(He explains. Perhaps his mother is sick.)
TEACHER: "What can we do to help Georgie?"
CHILDREN make suggestions:
  "Let's tell him a story."
  "Let's make a pretty card to send to his mother."
  "Let's make up a happy song for him."

"Let's tell him how we felt when our mother got sick."

(The teacher, too, tells how she felt.)

"Let's be especially kind to him today."

"Let's give him a hug."

Hugging should be encouraged: kids hugging each other, hugging the teacher, the teacher hugging the kids.

The recognition of sadness and joy and its causes can be taught to very young children. Remedies in the form of personal acts of kindness can also be taught. Attention should be payed to all acts of kindness and unkindness. We underestimate the ability of our children to understand mercy, sympathy, and generosity. Just as they can be taught that flowers are pretty and dresses are pretty, they can also be taught that behavior can be beautiful or ugly, sweet or sour, kind or unkind, just or unjust, tender or cruel. Self-expression includes what not to say as well as what to say, and what you say is more important than how well you say it. It is just as vital to approach the world with an open heart as with an open mind. Boys should not be taught that it is unmanly to cry. Men should not be ashamed to weep at injustice. When men will weep at the horrors of current history the world may become better. The world needs a good cry.

No lesson should end on the "right" answer. After the "right" answer to any problem is arrived at, is it too much to ask to what "good" is this "right" to be put? Every lesson should end in a moral and should answer the question "In what way, directly or indirectly, does this lesson make for better human beings, a better country, a better world?" The acquisition of facts and skills for their own sake is generally accepted as education. Knowledge can be destructive of all that the human race considers sacred. The soul needs as much education as the mind. Educators avoid the word "soul" simply because it is difficult to define in pedagogic terms. It is equally difficult to define "love," yet we all know when it is present.

Through all the years I taught Spanish in the high schools I wondered at what point the syllabus would include under the heading "Daily Life and Customs" subjects like hunger, tyranny and illiteracy, which in many Spanish-speaking countries are not minority but majority problems. What good does it do a young American to know the subjunctive if he feels no sympathetic pain for a foreign child of his own age who goes to bed hungry every night of his life? The travel posters on the classroom walls never showed such scenes. Who would travel three thousand miles to see a little girl with a twisted spine carrying her sickly little sister on her back? Let no child be called "educated" until he has seen and discussed the ugly pictures and made some moral commitment to the advancement of other human beings besides himself, a commitment not to be his brother's keeper, but his brother's brother.

The world has had its fill of educated brutes, "brilliant" men who have led great masses of people back to barbarism. I have seen as much personal cruelty among college professors as amongst illiterates. Personal inhumanity is not unusual in college departments which teach the "Humanities." I learned this at the tender age of twenty-one when my own college elected me to the Spanish Honor Society, but dissuaded me from applying for a full-time teaching position because the department "policy" at that time was opposed to "inbreeding," a policy which at that same time did not apply to qualified students of other faiths.

※※※※※

The high IQ has become the American equivalent of the Legion of Honor, positive proof of the child's intellectual aristocracy. The IQ is the intellectual credit card acceptable in any institution of learning from nursery school through college. The parents have also misused it with much harm to their children. Preschool children are being secretly trained for IQ tests by mothers who must have "superior" children. They have made the IQ a virtue unto itself, revered above character and the ability to live decently with people, qualities which do not have a number value. It has become more important to be a "smart kid" than a good kid or even a healthy kid.

There has been much amateur meddling with IQ scores. The proper interpretation of an IQ examination is a fine art. It should certainly not be left in the hands of the average parent or, for that matter, the average teacher. An individual IQ examination should be interpreted by an expert. As far as mass IQ tests are concerned, they have about as much personal validity as a mass cardiogram.

The IQ is only one aspect of individuality. While it generally indicates academic agility, any good educator will tell you it does not guarantee learning or academic success. Actual achievement very often contradicts the IQ grade, going above or below its prediction.

A high IQ certainly does not guarantee wisdom, intelligent application of knowledge to the problems of daily living, or sound values. I taught brilliant children who grew up to spend the precious hours of their mature life immersed in mediocrity, applying their keen learning ability only to the pursuit of the trivial and common-place.

We have all come into contact with half-bright Fulbrights, academic virtuosi who knock off scholarship after scholarship, grant after grant, degree after degree, who are in fact only full-grown infant prodigies frighteningly unintelligent in human relations. They are in perfect focus in front of a microscope, but out of focus with mankind. Sociology, yes, people, no; physiology, yes, the touch of a human hand, no. Such people have become so abstracted that they have forgotten that the basic text is human life.

I should also like to speak up for the intelligent slow child. This is not a contradiction in terms. Except for the child with a physically or emotionally impaired mind, a slow thinker is not necessarily a poor thinker. Too much intelligence testing is being done with stopwatch in hand. The quick answer has become the measure of intelligence. Speed is not a virtue in all areas. Some of the most creative minds in history have been slow thinkers. They have thought and re-thought and wondered and doubted, and their doubts have become milestones in the history of the human race.

I question, too, the cult of rapid reading. Is fast reading better reading? Some of the wisest people I have ever met are slow readers. They read slowly because they want to relish each word, enjoy it, taste it, smell it, challenge it, admire it. They love to read. This is good reading; not fast, but good.

⚙⚙⚙⚙⚙

There are many kinds of intelligence. At the moment, academic intelligence is being honored far above vocational intelligence. Only when the teachers and parents will come to truly believe it will the child also believe that his talent, whatever it is, is good, that he will be respected for his labors, that a job well done in any field of human endeavor is truly an achievement, whether it is cerebral or manual. Tribute is long overdue the future tillers, toilers, makers and menders who will keep our physical environment from falling apart at the seams.

We owe an apology to the nonacademically-minded young man who is not college bound. How often do the newspapers print the pictures of vocational school graduates who have made the most of their mechanical gifts? In June of each year long columns appear in the newspapers listing the names of the Westinghouse, Merit, and other scholarship winners. Rarely are the achievements of the vocational school youngsters similarly publicized. Why no fanfare for the future plumbers, painters, bakers, mechanics? We are not fooling the kids. Is the mechanic, by implication, a less important human being than the scientist? We keep on asking, "Who is going to do the plumbing?" Certainly not any young man whose honest labor is not respected as much as that of the scientist.

The members of juvenile gangs come mostly from the

ranks of the nonacademically-minded youngsters who resent their exclusion from places of honor reserved for the
"smart kids." In retaliation they create honor rolls of their
own, social orders in which they can achieve positions of
prestige. The very names of the street gangs indicate their
hunger for status: the Dukes, the Kings, the Royal Am-
bassadors, the Princes, the Lords, the Barons.

❀❀❀❀❀

Our schools have not given sufficient attention to the
fine arts as essential to the full development of the human
being. The cultivation of man's aesthetic nature is crucial
to our survival in a technological world. Music, art, and
the dance have as much to say about the human condition
as the sciences, yet the arts are generally offered as a minor
subject—a pleasant fringe benefit of compulsory education.
A recent survey in the New York City high schools indicated that less than 25 per cent of the schools assign their
students to required music classes on a daily basis for a
full term. The other schools expose their students to music
for one period per week for four terms, two periods per
week for two terms, or five periods per week for part of a
term. Besides, there is no fixed course of study for minor
music. To compound the felony, required music classes are
generally much larger than any other classes, with the
exception of gym.

Music is not generally regarded as a discipline. In the
New York high schools students are permitted to elect
major music and major art courses, taking classes five

times a week, but (1) they are considered half majors; (2) the grade earned is not always averaged in with the other major subjects. Most colleges, too, do not average in the grades in major music and art offered for college entrance. Taught correctly (and this cannot be done by people who have had two credits in How to Teach Music, but by professional musicians only), music is as much a discipline as mathematics. It involves as much logic, abstract thinking, concentration, imagination and academic know-how, and in addition it calls for physical coordination, emotional projection, self-expression and creativity.

The sympathetic vibrations stimulated by the sound of music may prompt the release of the child's personal message as well as do the so-called absolute sciences. The response to beauty is also evidence of knowledge. Feeling, too, is knowing.

We are reaping the harvest of aesthetic mediocrity sown by a long history of neglect of good music in the elementary schools and the smattering of "appreciation" in the high schools, which talks "about" music, but rarely involves the students' sensibilities. Such small doses of "culture" finally immunize young people against the real thing. Most American symphony orchestras cannot support themselves. Thousands of talented young musicians go unappreciated and unfulfilled, while musical illiterates make millions performing for other musical illiterates.

Because the schools have treated music as a minor, the rock 'n' roll purveyors can treat it as a major—a major industry built upon poor musical taste, poor aesthetic standards, and the emotional exploitation of our young. It sends out an army of song pluggers, record pluggers, promoters, fan-club organizers and spontaneous-ovation instigators, to capture the minds and allowances of the artistically innocent.

The rock 'n' roll industry knows how to teach "appreciation" better than the schools do. For about four years of their lives our brainwashed youngsters will swoon before the awesome presence of some sequin-jacketed, electronically amplified adolescent who became a howling success by just howling, a musical drop-out who rose to become the current high priest of a hi-fi fertility cult run by a syndicate of hysteria peddlers who know that this misguided minstrel is no musician, but want to keep him that way. Why take lessons, why study, when it's hip-shaking that pays off? A young "singer" is encouraged by his promoters to stake his life on a possible hit record that may flourish and die in about three weeks. After that he is neither educated nor a hit, but he will hang on for years in the hope of stumbling upon another hit. The industry favors luck over ability—a dangerous philosophy for young people.

The rock 'n' roll industry not only demands and gets maximum loyalty from its followers; it makes them hostile to any attempts to teach them good music in school. They look upon their teachers as "squares," and "long-hairs" who must be tolerated. If this teacher-guy were any good he'd have a hit record. "Hey, teacher. Is Chopin in the Top Ten? Play some of *our* music!"

While the rock 'n' roll business has a legal right to exploit our children for profit, I challenge their moral right. Our children will not be permanently maimed by all this exposure to musical junk, but I do regret that in the formative years of their lives so many will hear so little great music. All I ask is equal time on the radio and on TV for the Top Ten of great music, the eternals. When are they going to hear Schubert and Beethoven and Puccini? I have been told that they will get to know them later. There is no better time to get to know great art, great music, great books than in one's youth.

In the current American hierarchy of national heroes, baseball players, rock 'n' rollers, TV stars and movie stars rank very high. Teachers, artists and philosophers do not. The latter are still considered by the majority as "eggheads"—some with a double yolk.

The growing tendency in America of equating greatness with popularity (the highest attainment of the mass media) does injustice to men of quality. In my time I have witnessed the slow death of reverence. This is the age of the "regular guy." The closer the great man can be brought down to the average, the greater he is. He must not be above our immediate comprehension. Instead of raising the average man to an appreciation of the august, we cut heroes down to size.

Everyone, great or small, must be a "regular guy." The college president must be a good mixer. The spiritual head of a congregation must be able to listen to or even tell an off-color joke or lose his status as "one of the boys." A clergyman is auditioned by a committee of regular guys to make sure he's not "stuffy." He must present the right image: young, handsome, athletic and a good showman. He must also be a diplomat and stay away from controversial subjects like politics or religion. And his service mustn't be too long. "Make it short" are the usual last words of the parishioner who "hires" a clergyman.

No one requires a baseball player to go to concerts, but the great musician has to prove he is an "all right guy" by playing baseball. The greatest living Hamlet must trade insult jokes with the M.C. of a TV variety show and take a pie in the face, if necessary, to prove what a good sport he is. His play may close after a short run but last night on TV this "guy" was "great."

Sentiment is "corny." Deep feeling is "square." Great spiritual moments are "from Hicksville." Literary master-pieces are converted into comic books. The moment of silence has been cut down to five seconds. Ritual is staged. Photographers overrun religious ceremonies, banquet managers direct weddings, funeral directors produce inter-ments with corpses lighted by overhead ambers. It will not be long before all of life's memorable events will be listed in the Yellow Pages under Caterers.

We expose our young people to so many mock rituals that the genuine experience ultimately becomes meaning-less: cap-and-gown graduation exercises in nursery school, for example. As a result, fewer and fewer college graduates want to attend their own commencement exercises.

❋❋❋❋❋

How clearly and fearlessly have the schools spoken out against the enemies of education, not only against the out and out budget cutters, the it-was-good-enough-for-my-father citizens' groups, but against those other teachers, outside the schools, those who compete with the schools for the minds of our children, the mediocrity peddlers who sell their tawdry ideas and merchandise more successfully than the schools sell excellence?

After more than one hundred years of compulsory free education, are the schools ready to acknowledge that fewer than half the people in this country ever read a book once they have left school? That fewer than one out of five ever buy a book? That a recent Gallup poll reported that one out of ten college graduates could not name the authors of *An American Tragedy, Babbitt, The Canterbury Tales, Gulliver's Travels, Leaves of Grass, The Old Wives' Tale, Utopia, Vanity Fair, Origin of Species, The Wealth of Nations, The Rubaiyat,* and *Tom Jones?* (Four in ten could not name more than three.) That comic books sell to millions of children and adults (about thirty to forty million a month) who were and are our students? That the Beatles outsell Richard Tucker by the millions (The Beatles' take-home pay for one performance is larger than the combined salaries of the average public school faculty for one year)? That most high school students cannot name five living American symphonic composers or talk knowledgeably about five living American painters? That adult television shows with the lowest degree of intellectual stimulation, those guaranteed not to evoke anything but quick laughter and quick tears, have the highest rating among people who only yesterday were our students?

Those outside teachers who teach for profit know much about the psychology of learning. They can afford the motivational research that the schools can not. They know how the minds of their "students" function and know how to use this knowledge for gain.

The New York Times on August 15, 1965, included a 132-page paid advertising section called "Children's Fashions," an extremely clever document which employed the technique of a child's reader to inculcate sophisticated, materialistic, and often anti-intellectual attitudes in both children and parents in the interest of promoting the "correct" attitude toward the merchandise being sold. These ads reveal the fine hand of English majors. There's nothing like a background of creative writing for selling.

Here are some of the captions that came under the pretty pictures.

"How many (brand name) shirts do you see in this picture?"

"Can a boy have too many (brand name)? Impossible."

"A fairy-tale of fashion."

"Once upon a time there was a lovely piqué."

". . . make kids happy with in styling."

"The With-It-Kids."

"First edition for tiny swingers."

"What makes an egghead come out of his shell?"

"Pride. That's the feeling you have when you send the lambs on their way in outfits of pure virgin wool."

"It's a scientific world. Mixed prints and blazer stripes enliven any experiment."

"Happiness is going to school in outfits like these . . ."

"Lively imaginations can always find something to do at home; especially with the right outfit to do it in."

"————will assume no responsibility for campus riots or any other disturbance in the nation's schools that may be caused by excessive excitement over the———styles this fall."

Are the schools ready to face up to the fact that teen-age is not only an age bracket but one of America's largest consumer groups? That keeping up with the glamorous life expected of Miss Teen-age America costs her group about twenty-five million dollars a year for deodorants, about twenty million a year for lipstick, about nine million for home permanents, and undetermined amounts on underground (transistor) radios on which they get their orders so that these millions of nonconformists can nonconform together? By 1970 some 55 per cent of the nation's consumer-students will be in the under-twenty-five bracket.

While cosmetics are no longer considered vulgar or the sign of the fallen woman, do the schools have the courage to tell our teen-age daughters that they need them like they need a hole in the head? Any school kid who makes up as though she were going to take a screen test for the role of Cleopatra should be told to wash her face and let the natural loveliness of youth shine through. Better to live with a few pimples of her own than with the mask of a stranger. I don't think it is the province of the school to run beauty clinics for fourteen-year-old *femmes fatales.* The schools might teach that intellectual curiosity makes the eyes bright, that kind words make the lips attractive, that bending over to help your neighbor makes the blood rush to the cheeks and does wonder for the complexion.

What happens to the youngster who has no money but is still exposed to an unremitting barrage of propaganda about his "needs" in order to be "in"? For many the need becomes so consuming they will take what they cannot buy.

When the school is at a loss to explain student hostility (ranging from disrespect to vandalism) it falls back upon "The parents are guilty. They don't teach them." We forget that the parents, too, are the product of our schools. What did the schools fail to teach the hostile parents of hostile children? Did we really teach them or did we just have them in class?

Are the schools today the victims of too many years of their own nonresistance, their own meek conformism, their own equivocal status as leaders in American society, their tacit abdication of the role of uncompromising teacher-defender of the great truths of civilization?

There is a pedagogic axiom which states that the school must reflect society. It should do much more. The school must improve society. Free compulsory education was intended as an instrument for social improvement. The teacher should by definition be a reformer. When the environment corrupts it is not enough to explain how this happens; the school must strive to change the environment. If the environment makes some students unteachable the teacher must come to grips with the environment. It is not easy. Courageous teachers who raise their voices often end up having their loyalty questioned. Eventually they retreat to the three Rs, carefully omitting the mention of the fourth R—responsibility—personal and collective. For too long teachers have been intimidated into accepting the world beyond the schoolyard as none of their concern.

How so many teachers manage to retain a high level of professional devotion under the existing pressures is remarkable and a tribute to their idealism. The teachers' colleges train the prospective teacher to see the "whole child." This is a neat trick if you can see the child at all through the paperwork, the endless forms and reports to be filled out; the monies to be collected for drives, field trips, ball games, buses, lunches; the notes from and to home, from and to dentists, from and to doctors, not to mention such pedagogic functions as nose wiping, zipper unjamming, measles detection, lost-child finding, angry-mother appeasing.

It is possible that the high incidence of hostility among deprived children and their parents derives from a long-smoldering resentment against the public schools for having let them down for several generations. They would have liked the school to be, above all, a sanctuary from social hypocrisy. They wanted the miserable truths of their lives recognized in school.

To many culturally and economically deprived youngsters the school environment is unreal. It certainly does not embrace their environment. The child's primers deal with a world in which there is no poverty, no tears, no hunger, and no minority problems. Maybe Johnny can't read because he doesn't *want* to read what from his point of view is a fairy tale, a story about a happy father in a neat business suit coming home to his happy little family in a snug little cottage, greeted by the happy little puppy. "Jump, dog, jump." "Smile, Dick, smile." This is a world beyond the reaches of this child's experience and imagination.

My own first schoolbooks were equally incredible. (It was the educational strength of my home that overcame them.) I, too, wondered what world those textbook kids lived in. My father didn't come home from work smiling. He didn't go to work smiling, either. Most of the time there was no work to go to or come back from. Nor was my mother a Smiling Suzy in a white apron. She got up every morning in the dark and groaned through the drudgery of an endless day into the dark of another night. We were not two cute little children, but eight, and we didn't stand around grinning like fools.

Our house was not a cottage small by a waterfall, but a tenement large by a sewer leak. And we didn't go on happy picnics to the country—"Look, rabbit, look." Never mind the rabbit. Look at me! Dogs didn't say "Bow-wow." They went mad with the heat and bit kids who were on the streets instead of in school where they should have been, singing "I'll Sing Thee Songs of Araby, and Tales of Fair Kashmir."

Until very recently, and even then only in a few "pilot" cities (usually those in which violence has broken the sound barrier of middle-class silence), most Negro children never saw a picture of a Negro child in a primer. The dark-skinned child felt deliberately excluded. By the time he reached junior high school he began to suspect that there had been much glossing over the facts of *his* life, that his teacher was part of a conspiracy of silence, or worse, part of a total deception perpetrated by society.

The unrecognized child ultimately loses faith in both home and school. He has not found himself in either place. He is drop-out material. Did he drop us, or, in truth, did we drop him? As far as the boy is concerned, it is too late. The street gang has a vocabulary he understands.

Shoot, Dick, shoot; Stab, Dick, stab. He laughs at the naïve attempts of the social worker to "rehabilitate" him. Now, at last, he is truly well-adjusted to his environment—the environment the curriculum politely ignored. From here on in he learns about life from the example of the elders of his community—the alumni association of the disinherited and disillusioned. The teacher, who might have been his salvation, adhered too closely to the alien text and alienated the child.

Textbooks everywhere (in middle- and upper-class communities as well as in the slums) should reflect the cultural and ethnic pluralism of our country. Some school systems (New York, Detroit, Chicago, and a few others) have demonstrated the effectiveness of multicultural primers (not books which include a chapter on the contribution of the minorities, nor even a Negro Who's Who on the reference shelf of the library, nor books on Negro history —these are too difficult and often too late to do much good), but beginning readers populated by children of various races. Where such books have been used the youngsters have shown an increased desire as well as ability to read. The child not only recognizes words, he recognizes *himself* in those words. Is this not what the great educators had in mind when they talked of reaching the child in terms of his interests?

Some deprived children are utterly lacking in self-identification. They have never even seen a photograph of themselves. Understanding teachers who know how much these children's egos need reinforcement have taken pictures of each child and pasted them on his desk next to a mirror, which was also placed there so that the child might see himself as others do.

Color has generally been taught as a property of things, or sometimes of animals. The book is red; the bear is black. The concept of color in people has to be introduced to children at the same time as the color of things, so that color comes to be accepted in people and things as just another identifying characteristic. "Jack is white, Dick is black, roses are red, violets are blue. Our flag is red, white, and blue. Our flag has many colors. Children have many colors. George has red hair. Mary has black hair. Ethel has white skin. Freddie has black skin. Color this boy black. Color this apple red. Color this girl brown."

Many educators are beginning to recognize the fact that most so-called intelligence tests (usually standardized on the basis of tests given to groups in which no Negroes or other minorities were included) are not valid for the culturally deprived child, whose language and general frame of reference are so meager as to guarantee a low grade. The label of "below average" becomes a permanent part of the school record that follows the child through the years, reminding him and his teachers of his proven "innate" inferiority—an inferiority which conscientious, as well as conscience-stricken educators have been able to disprove by special nonverbal tests.

Verbal fluency seems to be lacking in the culturally impoverished. The nonverbal tests are administered orally. They require no reading at all. In their creation, consideration was given to geographical location, parental occupation and racial background. Until such time as many more tests of this kind are available, New York City has abandoned the group intelligence test in favor of an observation guide to be used by teachers for recording an emotional and intellectual profile of the individual child.

Grouping kids in classrooms on the basis of mental-ability test scores at the time of admission to school leads to segregation and the perpetuation of the same conditions which in the outer world have depressed the minds of so many children. Coexistence of a variety of cultural backgrounds in the same classroom seems to do them all good. For this to be truly effective, however, the class must be kept small.

It may be too late to help the parents, but there is still time to save the current crop of youngsters and break the cycle of ineducability. We have finally come forward with compensatory programs like Head Start, which attempt to correct the cultural limp which has prevented some children from keeping pace with the others. The school, at long last, is going to provide the culturally handicapped child with an intensive preschool program from the age of three to six which it is hoped will bring him up to the level of the child who comes from a more culturally advanced home. Perhaps we shall be able to prove that it is not the child who is backward, but the society that neglected him.

In order to meet the needs of all the children colleges will have to train prospective teachers in the science of human relations, with emphasis on minority and poverty problems. Most teachers need this training, since most of them come from nice, stable, middle-class homes, and have had their practice teaching in such communities.

Many teachers come psychologically unprepared for the resentment they will find in many localities. They are often frustrated by their inability to penetrate the emotional barricade the child has erected against them. Even the best-intentioned teacher may sometimes become unconsciously hostile toward such a child. Efforts are now being made to recruit teachers who are "in-migrants," alumni of the problem areas, young men and women who have lived with the problems these children are now facing and have overcome them. All who are going to teach in these areas should serve an internship in the community outside of the classroom in order to become acquainted with the realities of life there. More male teachers are needed in areas where fatherless homes are common.

To establish better communication between teachers and children we need home visiting by teachers, for their own enlightenment and for the enlightenment of the parents. The schools, naturally, must allow time for such visits as essential to the business of teaching and not try to squeeze them in as an extra added attraction.

At least forty-five minutes of each day should be devoted to the discussion of subjects of local interest suggested by the students in order to bridge the gap between their world and the school world. Unpleasant subjects like rats, falling plaster, narcotics, cockroaches, and (with older students) prostitution, poolrooms, and numbers peddlers should not be avoided. Along with the examination of teeth, eyes and throat, there should be regular check-ups for narcotics addiction.

No teacher with less than five years' experience should

be assigned to problem areas. Teachers should volunteer for such assignments. An unwilling teacher could only do harm.

The entire concept of what a school building should look like and the kind of services it must be equipped to provide will have to change. The public school should serve the public's every educational need, even if it has to stay open day and night fifty-two weeks a year. This is the building to which the community should be able to bring all educational, vocational and legal problems involving their children, including part-time and full-time employment. The various Government youth agencies should function out of the school building.

There does come a time, however, when some high school youngsters have proven themselves unreachable for a variety of reasons. To make continued attendance in school compulsory for such young people is the equivalent of imposing a prison sentence. At this point, formal education should stop and the labor unions should move in to fill the void between school and job. As the avowed champions of the working people, they will have to see to it that the young man whose personal message is destined to be delivered through manual labor be given the tools, the time, and the place. Employment insurance is better than unemployment insurance.

If automation has brought us to the point where there are, in fact, fewer and fewer jobs each year (we need almost two million new jobs per year to take care of our young men and women), we should admit this, too, and stop giving false hopes to young people. They have been disillusioned too often.

Economic self-sufficiency should be one of the basic aims of education in a democratic society. Gainful employment is a joyful experience. Honest work has moral value. One's self-esteem is firmly established when the world is willing to pay for your services; skilled, semi-skilled or unskilled. Every man must ultimately be inducted into the economic fraternity as a contributing member. In a responsible society there must be no such thing as a total drop-out. When a youngster leaves school he should be able to choose between two exits—one marked TO WORK, and the other TO MORE EDUCATION. There should be no exit leading TO NOWHERE, and certainly no unguarded exits. It is not just a living we are responsible for but a life.

What, after all, is education? The dictionary definition is: "To bring up a child physically or mentally; to educate. Also: to develop and cultivate mentally or morally; to expand, strengthen and discipline the mind, or a faculty, etc. To prepare and fit for any calling or business by systematic instruction; to cultivate; train; instruct. Synonym: Develop, teach, inform, enlighten, indoctrinate.

It follows, therefore, that it becomes the duty of *all* who educate to remove the obstacles—psychological, physical, emotional, intellectual or environmental—which might undermine this definition.

I am sure that the story is apocryphal, but it is told that someone asked Michelangelo what method he used for sculpting his Moses. "It is very simple," he is credited as saying. "You just take a chunk of marble and chop away everything that doesn't look like Moses."

The implication is clear: that within any crude piece

of stone (or child) lies a work of art, if you know what to chop away in order to reveal it.

It should also be emphasized that the child will have to help with the chopping. Discovering ones self is hard work.

SSSSS

The founding fathers said: "All men are endowed by their Creator with certain inalienable rights."

Christianity says: "The Lord make you to increase and abound in love one toward another and toward all men."

Judaism says: "What thou thyself hatest, do to no man."

Confucianism says: "What you do not want done to yourself, do not do unto others."

Islam says: "Help one another in righteousness and piety."

How, against this background of lofty principles to which all men pretend to subscribe, do we explain to our children the petty hatreds, slurs, restrictions and humiliations inflicted upon those singled out as "undesirables" by self-appointed "desirables"?

Of all obstacles to a human being's growth to full stature prejudice is the worst. It destroys more individuals than war. It is hereditary, not in the blood stream, but in the stream of conversation within the home. Out of the mouths of babes come adult slanders, repeated word for word.

How do you go about explaining to your child the meaning of words like spick, dago, wop, sheenie, kike, nigger, hunk, polack, shanty, mockie, hebe, chink, coon, greaser? You might refer him to some glossary where he will get nice, sterile definitions with all the pain removed, or you might refer him to a living victim with the pain still in him.

What a horror it must be for a child to discover that his skin is the wrong color. How can he liberate himself from the despised skin? Of all disadvantages, this, the terrible disadvantage of color, was the one my brothers and I did not have to overcome. A child learns early in life that color hatred is not just skin deep. It goes clear through to the marrow of his self-esteem. Hate my skin, hate me. Often he comes to accept his oppressor's judgment and ends up hating himself and his group. What an iniquity in a civilized world to burden a newborn child with the hatred of ages.

Society has no right to mislead any child by promising him rewards for good conduct which it will not deliver. If he is treated like the experimental guinea pig in the maze he will behave like the guinea pig. A reward, usually a piece of cheese, is placed at the end of the tricky passageway. The guinea pig will make hundreds of learning attempts until he finally finds the right road to the reward. However, if after he has succeeded in learning the right road, you remove the cheese, even a guinea pig can have a nervous breakdown or become violent. The child who makes every effort to learn the "right way," who strains to achieve the reward only to find it cynically withdrawn at the last moment, will break down. If we offer a reward for virtue we must offer it without consideration of skin color, language or religion, or we will reap the reward of violence.

This aberration called prejudice is an ancient malady and no one is completely immune to it. Even those most often victimized by prejudice may nurture prejudices of their own, perpetuating the vicious cycle of unreasoning, sick hate: white against black, black against white, nation against nation, neighborhood against neighborhood, man against man.

Prejudice makes sneak border raids. The English, for example, say, "He took French leave." The French say, "He took English leave." Venereal disease, politely referred to in America as V.D., is called by Italians and Icelanders "French disease"; the French call it "The Prussians"; the Germans call it "Spanish Pox"; the Portuguese call it the "Neapolitan disease."

The other fellow has wrong ideas, bad manners, big feet, a hard head, big eyes, a fat belly; he is too intelligent, too shrewd, too dumb, too rich, too poor, too different. Very often prejudice exists where you would not expect it—within an ethnic or national group itself: Napolitano vs. Siciliano, West Indian Negro vs. American Negro, Litvak vs. Galitsianer, North vs. South, City vs. Country, Uptown vs. Downtown, Old American vs. New American.

In the folklore of prejudice all Irishmen are drunks, all Jews are rich, all Poles are dumb, all Scotsmen are stingy, all Negroes are lazy, all Italians smell of garlic. Many Orientals think that white people smell bad. When the Chinese gentleman visiting America was asked what he found most odd about Americans, he said, "The peculiar slant of their eyes."

Throughout American history each new immigrant group was met by "anti-bodies." When the Irish came to

America in search of freedom and bread, discrimination was waiting on the shore. Some Irish old-timers may remember a song that was popular when they came to this country:

> I'm a dacint boy, just landed from the town of Ballyfad
> I want a situation—yes, and want it mighty bad.
> I have seen employment advertised
> " 'tis just the thing," says I,
> But the filthy spalpeen ended with
> "No Irish need apply."

The violated minority can appeal for justice but the final solution of the problem will have to come from the oppressor. Basically, anti-Semitism is a Christian problem. The Negro problem must finally be solved by the white man. After all, who done it?

Shedding a prejudice is an agonizing experience. An illogical hatred nourished for hundreds of years for whatever reason—religious, economic, or political—finally becomes a mass mental disease. The white people of this country are predominantly favorable to the Negro's demands for equality, yet many cannot shed their prejudice. When they say "The Negro is not ready yet," what they mean is "I am not ready yet."

It will take longer to unravel the knots of hatred in the white man than it will to achieve equality for the Negro. I have heard white men of good will say: "I don't want to hate him. I hate myself for hating him. I don't know why I hate him." One woman's deep-rooted fear of the Negro came to this: "Who is *she* to hate me? I am somebody.

When she becomes somebody I will be nobody. If she moves next door we all become nobody. We can't all be somebody."

I am concerned here primarily with the effect of prejudice on the chances of the newborn babe delivering his message to the world. What are the odds for a kid born with the unpopular skin of the century? How can we afford the possible loss of this child's talents, one of which may lead to a cure for cancer, or perhaps even a cure for the greatest killer of them all—prejudice? What might happen to the world if for one generation we did not teach our children to hate?

☼☼☼☼☼

Getting lost is an experience all of us have gone through as children. If you can recall the terror of losing your mother in a crowd, of finding yourself in a world of strange and hostile faces, with the sure knowledge that you would never again find your way home, tormented, in addition, by the suspicion that this was not an accident at all but a deliberate desertion on the part of your mother; if you can recall how you turned down the help of strangers, how you even struck out at kindly people who touched you because you would accept nothing less than the return of your mother, you may be able to understand the juvenile delinquent acting out the Negro spiritual "Sometimes I feel like a motherless child, a long way from home."

For the young man on the verge of maturity, severe panic sets in as he realizes that somewhere in the continuing rumble he has lived in he has lost the message he was born to deliver to the world. The fist that held a message when he was born now holds a knife with which he seeks to avenge himself against a world that allowed this to happen.

The child's need for home is so elemental that children placed in public institutions far superior to the home they were being raised in break out to "go home." They are always willing to forgive their parents and give them another chance.

The juvenile delinquent is made, not born. A delinquent child from a good home and an upright child from a bad home are both exceptions. I am amazed not that we have so many delinquent children but, in view of the meager leadership our generation has offered its young, that we do not have more.

🏵🏵🏵🏵

There is a type of alleged "broadmindedness" rampant in America that tolerates just about anything, including murder. Is it broadmindedness, moral apathy, or just plain cowardice? Minding one's business has become a virtue. If you see a kid behaving like a hoodlum you say to yourself, "It's not my kid, so it's not my problem." Personally, I'm for snitching. Delinquency is *our* problem. When it is for the common good, snitching is good. My mother was a snitcher, as were all the other mothers in our neighborhood. If I ever did anything wrong, by the time I got home my mother knew about it via the maternal grapevine. The snitch-scouts had turned me in. I would be grateful to any mother who came to me and told me of any misbehavior on the part of my children. Snitching should be reinstated as a form of collective discipline. We might also revive Mama's type of Mother's Club, whose platform was: "Parents of America, unite. Join, the UPA —Unafraid Parents of America. Join a club, or even better, bring a small one of your own."

When Mama and her gang staged a guerrilla raid on the neighborhood poolroom, even the bookies took to the rooftops. The women would grab cue sticks and swing out wildly smashing bulbs and heads. The mamas who couldn't join the gang (those usually in the last stages of pregnancy) deputized others to act for them: "If you see my bum in the poolroom, kill him. I'll do the same for you."

"Thank you."

"Don't mention it."

"God bless you."

"Such a nice lady."

The Billiard Academy finally lost the battle against the Vigilante Mothers and had to move to a better neighborhood. A truck pulled up and carted away the pool tables in the presence of a gang of cheering mothers. Some two hundred potential gangsters were left without party headquarters.

I guess I shall never get used to the sight of children out on the streets late at night. To this day, when I find myself out late, I expect to see my mother turning the corner to greet me with "Hey, bum, you looking for trouble? Come on home and I'll give you some."

One night—it must have been about 2 A.M.—I passed a

corner where a gang of teen-agers was congregated, and no mama in sight. Obviously no one cared enough for these boys to lead them home. I got out of my car, walked up to a policeman and asked, "What are these kids doing out so late?" "They're not doing anything illegal," was the polite but curt reply. I recognized the "Mind your own business" implicit in his tone of voice.

True, they weren't breaking any law. Fortunately for me and all my brothers, staying out late on the streets was in itself considered a breach of a moral law laid down by elders who felt it was easier to forestall trouble than to mop up after it.

Mama had a method for keeping you from going out at night that was charmingly disarming. She would ask questions until you either lost interest or it was too late to go. "Where are you going? Where is Park Avenue? Near what street? What kind of name is that for a street? He's your friend? Who's his mother? Is he an honest boy? What does his father do? Who ever heard of a trade like that? How long do you know him? Do you know what time it is? Who goes anywhere so late? Go to bed better." Every hour after 10 P.M. was four o'clock in the morning. "Do you know when he got home? Four o'clock in the morning."

In the name of "understanding" we have abandoned our children to their own devices and rules in the belief that uncompromising stands taken by parents will cause irreparable traumas in their offspring. Our young, on the other hand, are waiting for us to make up our minds. The teen-ager has to cope with two sets of confusions—his and ours. The parents are as shook up as the kids. Given time the kids will become as befuddled and inconsistent as their parents. They are almost afraid to become adults in a world in which adults cannot make up their own minds about what is worth living for.

Family life in my parents' home seemed to us to be based upon a cosmic order: Papa was the sun, Mama the moon, and we kids the satellites. A child could not be a major planet; a father naturally was. We each gave or received light, warmth and direction according to our relationship to each other. Individually we understood our place, our space, our proper distance, and it all seemed to make sense.

In our family, as in the universe, there were eclipses, cold and warm seasons, clashes that rocked the heavens, and stars that fell and died. We accepted our roles in the family cosmos until we were old enough and strong enough to go out and establish an order of our own. For a system which would seem to have been so highly preordained and constrictive, we were a pretty independent and creative lot of kids. During the years the boys were planning and working toward a place in the sun for themselves they found great comfort and stability in the strength of our ordered existence.

The maintenance of a healthy family life rested upon Mama, who never rested. The world we live in now guarantees parents many freedoms which it did not guarantee to Mama. She had willingly traded her freedom for a greater good: order and dignity in the home.

While it is virtually impossible, willingly or unwillingly, for parents today to imitate Mama's way of life, it would still be wise for anyone contemplating marriage to be forewarned that one's freedom will be radically curtailed by the demands of parenthood. No one should get married until he is ready to give up many liberties. The needs of the children, while they should not always come first, must be considered. The children, on the other hand, should learn early in life that freedom is not absolute for them, either; that just as the parent must do what must be done for the common good, so must the children; that the family structure is a mutual corporation called Freedom, Ltd., in which each member of the family has a share. The more conscientious the parent, the smaller his share of freedom.

My parents weren't always right, but they were clear. They figured that if they didn't teach us someone else would. In a moment of choice between right and wrong I could hear the echoes of their oft-repeated admonitions in my inner ear—"nagging" is what they would call it today. Their position had been unequivocally stated and consistently maintained on what they believed was proper concerning dating, marriage, smoking, drinking, cosmetics, manners, hours, money, clothing, elders, play, teachers, books, dancing, lying, cheating, driving, clubs, sex, errands, movies, jobs, homework, punishment, obedience, friends, cleanliness, language, truancy, study. . . .

The need for clarity and consistency is even greater today when our teen-agers are offered more temptations and opportunities for messing up their lives than we had. Sometimes these opportunities are euphemistically labeled "advantages."

Kids in conflict with the community fall into two basic groups: those who got too much too soon, and those who got too little too late. The too much and the too little are not to be measured in terms of material offerings alone. The child, rich or poor, bereft of love and a decent family life is indeed deprived. Economic poverty alone does not produce delinquency. If it did my brothers and sister and I should all have become gangsters, as should most people in the world, since most of the world is poor. Why, then, is there virtually no juvenile delinquency in New York's Chinatown? Why is there juvenile delinquency in wealthy suburbia?

Any child who is lucky enough to be born into a disciplined home is already in possession of the greatest "advantage." Discipline has become a dirty word in recent years. It implies corporal punishment and parental dictatorship. A child needs discipline as much as a young plant needs care in order to grow. Parents will forcefully pin down a child when he is getting a shot of penicillin "for his own good," but, when strength is required for a moral shot in the rear they become powerless.

Parents today shrink from the unpleasant duty of disciplining their children for fear that they may lose their love. Actually it works in reverse. The child who is disciplined feels loved. The intractable child may be suffering from too much "It's up to you, darling." The parent who feels he must have the approval of his children at all times has abdicated the role of parent and becomes a frightened child himself. The child's recalcitrance is often a test of his parent's right to be head of the family. The tribe needs a chief. A good, healthy battle of the minds between parents and children is of great therapeutic value to both sides. It takes great courage and foresight to say as my father did: "I don't care what you think of me now; I am concerned with what you will think of me twenty years from now." It takes even greater courage to say: "Better that the children should cry than the parents." Ask any Juvenile Court judge how many convicted children have parted from their weeping parents with an indicting "Why didn't you stop me?" Sooner or later the child rebukes the parent for not having compelled him to do the right thing, whether it had to do with music practice or homework or companions, with "Why did you listen to me? I was only a kid."

Making a child unhappy today in the interest of a better tomorrow requires a stout heart. Happiness, if it comes at all, comes after the solution of problems, after the conquest of obstacles. We must all serve time at hard labor before we become free. Celebration comes after victory, not before. There are too many youngsters celebrating without cause.

I sometimes wonder whether the pedagogues haven't overdone the learning-can-be-fun-concept in teaching. Learning by doing is one thing. There is a danger that making a game of every lesson will develop a playboy attitude toward education.

A principal I know visited a classroom. He saw the teacher hold up a card that said "Run"—and thirty-seven kids ran wildly all around the room and into each other. Then another card: "Fall"—and they fell all over each other. Then "Hop" and they hopped all over each other. When the principal asked what was going on, the teacher said, "We're having a reading lesson."

We are also suffering from the delusion that a beautiful school building guarantees better learning. This is known among educators as the "edifice complex."

Learning is not always fun. It is also drudgery, discomfort, strain and anxiety. These, too, are important "learn-ing experiences" which a child must recognize, or he will come to shy away from hard work of any kind. Real thinking is a strenuous business, but the reward of knowl-edge gained through conscious effort is a true joy.

Thomas H. Huxley said, "Perhaps the most valuable re-sult of all education is the ability to make yourself do the thing you have to do, when it ought to be done, whether you like it or not. . . ." If the work to be done in the world had to depend upon people being "in the mood" very little work would ever get done. Work, once started, creates a mood of its own.

❈❈❈❈

When a community hires a teacher it makes clear what standards of conduct are becoming to his position. In gen-eral the teacher is expected to be a paragon of virtue: pure, noble, incorruptible, upright, sober, law-abiding, principled, just, unbiased, high-minded.

The parent is a teacher, too, but there is no written agreement between him and society. He teaches by exam-ple. Very often the parent, in all innocence, looks at his child and asks, "Where does he learn such things?" The answer is that he learned most of them at home when:

1. Mom signed that phony note to school explaining the child's absence "on account of illness" so she could go shopping with Mommy.

2. Dad said, "Money is the answer to everything."

3. Mom said that the teacher was a crackpot. (Teachers, being human, can do wrong. I know because I was and I

did, but this should never be told to the child. Respect for the teacher is an indispensable factor in the learning process. Any difference between the parent and the teacher should be settled behind closed doors and never in the presence of the child.)

4. Dad congratulated his son on "finding" that five-dollar bill without bothering to check on his good luck.

5. Dad "helped him" with his homework by doing it for him.

6. Dad told him, You're only young once, and now is the time for sowing wild oats (as long as they don't sprout on Dad's front lawn).

7. Dad told him that all you need to succeed in America is pull.

If there are any lessons in corruption the child has not picked up around the house during the day, he can tune in the evening news on TV and witness the greatest adult crimes of our generation—the peacetime wars all over the world, the "unofficial" killing of hundreds of human beings per day avowedly in order to improve their lives.

In some communities an attempt has been made to ease the resentment of the teen-agers against the adults, half of whom are telling him to find himself, and the other half to get lost. Instead of making secret treaties with their own teen-agers, the parents of these communities (suburban Philadelphia, Pennsylvania, Niagara Falls, New York, Summit, New Jersey, to name a few) have made a concerted effort to clarify and improve parent-teen-ager-school relations. While the method was not identical in all cases, it followed this general pattern: The parents met separately in the evening at school and drew up what they thought was a reasonable set of rules of conduct. The youngsters also held sessions and came to conclusions of their own. Then the two groups came together and discussed the suggested code item by item. The code was finally published at the expense of either the PTA or some local civic organization, and a copy given to each student.

It is interesting to note that those rules which most parents thought the teen-agers would never accept were in fact voted in and lived up to by the majority. Some teenagers even thought the codes were not tough enough.

Since most teen-agers like to belong to the "in" group, the establishment of these codes made it possible for all to be "in." It also made the parents happy to be "in," too.

In these codes there seems to be common agreement on the following: Going steady before graduation from high school is usually listed under "Discouraged Activities." Mixed parties are not to start before the eighth and ninth grades and are to be confined to school, community or religious groups, under adult supervision. Evening social activities are limited to weekends and holidays, never on an evening preceding a school day. Boy-girl baby-sitting teams are out. Baby-sitting and dating must be separate events. Home parties are permitted only when the parents are at home. "Lights out" is out at all parties. Drinking of any liquor is out at all times. Smoking is also on the "to be discouraged" list.

The time for the beginning and the end of parties is to be announced beforehand, and no one leaves a party except to go home. To simplify matters even more, the hour of homecoming from weekend socials is arranged not by age but by grade in school:

GRADE	HOME BY
7th	9:00
8th	9:30
9th	10:30
10th	11:00
11th	11:00
12th	12:00

For that extra-special "please, Ma" event, the schedule may be advanced by a half hour.

Parents are to be told where their children are going and with whom. Children must also know where their parents are at all times. In all fairness to the children, we must point out that many youngsters do not want to go home or stay home because they don't like to be there alone. In some communities it is easier to get the children off the streets than the parents. One community agency made a telephone survey calling a sampling of homes to ask the question: "Do you know where your children are tonight?" In at least half the cases the children were at home but didn't know where their parents were. You don't have to be a juvenile to be a delinquent. It is possible for a child to be justifiably ashamed of his parents. Parents, go home!

❋❋❋❋❋

Too many parents are making moral decisions for themselves and their children on the basis of a dubious criterion which has sneaked up on us imperceptibly through the years and now colors our personal as well as our public lives. Instead of boldly asking ourselves, "What good can it do?" we are willing to settle for "What harm can it do?" The individual family, like the family of man, can absorb only a limited amount of "harmless" poisons without ill effect, after which decay sets in and the harm is here to stay.

What harm is there in a group of kids hanging around a street corner at 2 A.M.? What harm is there in a teenager's taking a drink or two? What harm in the after-prom date that runs until 6 A.M.? What harm in taking a ride in a car you don't own? What harm in joining a gang just for kicks?

In many instances the areas of "good" and "harm" are separated only by the railroad tracks. If wealthy teen-agers borrow a car and go joy riding, they're just "living it up a little." Rich boys are "mischievous"; poor boys are "hoodlums." The vandalism of children in the "better" communities is often hushed up through the cooperation of the families and authorities.

Drink is no longer the "curse of the working class." I've been to parties in wealthy homes where girls in pigtails were sipping cocktails and everybody thought they were cute as all get-out. I've seen ten-year-old kids tending bar, rigged up in a bartender's apron, much to the delight of their sophisticated parents. These kids were swallowing in their father's footsteps. Getting "tight" is just another aspect of our fun-morality.

Teen-age drinking, like teen-age smoking, is an attempt to alter one's personality, to substitute apparent sophistication for hidden immaturity. It indicates displeasure with one's self and the attempt to create a new self. Young people who know and respect themselves do not need to drown themselves. The kid who must hide behind a screen of cigarette smoke has problems greater than his smoking habit. He is usually an immature, nervous youngster whose "manly" pose is a cover-up for failures in school, relationships with his peers, his parents, and authority in general. (When I was in my early nicoteens I knew that smoking would shorten my life—especially if Mama caught me.)

There is nothing sacred about trends. A new custom is not necessarily a good custom even if it is "nationwide." Take the vogue of planned sloppiness in dress, for instance. Any red-blooded teenager caught with his shoes shined today would be court-martialed by a jury of his peers and sentenced to pressed pants for life. When in a moment of ill-advised tolerance the schools succumbed to this trend they invited trouble. Psychologists have pointed out that there is a positive correlation between clothing and mental attitude. Sloppy dress encourages sloppy behavior. An institution of learning has the right to expect a little more decorum than a bowling alley. No one would "come as you are" to religious services. Why are two-tone shoes (white and dirt) and socks at half-mast acceptable at school?

Some of the teen-age girls underdress. The discovery of the newly arrived charms of her body often lead the figure-happy youngster to display her wares too freely. She becomes both an attraction and a distraction. Whether she knows it or not, and most likely she does, this get-up is a come-on to the boys. In the slanguage of her colleagues "she's asking for it."

One very fine junior high school near my home presents all incoming students with the following rules for school dress: girls may not wear chino pants, fatigue pants, dungarees, jeans, levis, shorts, pedal pushers, culottes, off-the-shoulder blouses, kerchiefs, curlers in the hair. Boys may not wear T shirts. If they wear jersey shirts they should have collars and look like shirts, not undershirts.

I should like to make a radical suggestion that might help solve the problem of the mother who finds it expensive to keep her children well dressed, as well as the problem of the mother whose daughter constantly needs new dresses for school because "the girls saw this dress already." I should like to propose school uniforms for all children. I am aware of the fact that many parochial and private schools do this. On first thought, it sounds like regimentation and destruction of individuality. The fact is that in many countries just as civilized as ours students wear attractive uniforms embroidered with their school insignia. They can be very colorful. The child is pleased to be recognized as a "student," an honor in itself. The wearing of an identifiable school uniform also influences personal behavior, since the child wishes to bring credit to his school wherever he appears in public.

※※※※※

In tribal cultures, when a youth successfully survives the *rites de passage,* he is granted the status of manhood and a wife of his own. In middle-class America he gets a car. "Spare the rod" today means simply that the young man has a date, as in "Can you spare the rod tonight, Dad?" If he has no car he doesn't stand much of a chance of getting a wife and starting a subtribe of his own.

Walking with a girl as a form of courting is archaic. "May I carry you and your books home from school in my car, Nancy?"

"Thank you, Georgie, but Freddie has a better car."

Some of the suburban high schools look like country clubs. Teachers now have the additional chore of patrolling the parking lot. The newest excuse for coming late to class is: "I couldn't find a place to park."

Statistics gathered by educators in various parts of the country indicate that oil and marks don't mix. All surveys seem to agree that as the curve of teen-age driving goes up, the curve of scholarship goes down. You can't be in two places nor serve two masters at the same time. There also seems to be a high correlation between teen-age car ownership and discipline problems.

Some parents feel that if the boy earns the money to pay for and support a car he has a right to it. Actually boys don't own cars; cars own boys. The car becomes a consuming interest and an expensive one.

In cases where the car is a family necessity it should belong to the parents. When the boy proves himself morally and emotionally responsible he may take the car out under safety rules, time limits and geographic boundaries agreed upon by the parents.

The car is also an ideal vehicle of escape. For young people it provides a perfect way of getting away from it all, and them all. It provides that kind of privacy and freedom not readily available at home, where adults are always hanging around. It is a home away from home. A car often doubles as a mobile boudoir. More girls have been converted in convertibles in the last twenty years than in bedrooms during the previous hundred years. But, say you, "I trust my daughter." And I say there are conditions under which even Grandma, driven to the right drive-in, just might be driven to it.

We are concerned here not with cars as such, but with the effect that all material acquisitions have upon the moral health of our children and of ourselves. As the environment provides more and more things, we must act as a Bureau of Standards to pass on the influence of things on moral values.

❀❀❀❀❀

The gap between dating and mating is being rapidly narrowed. This development, part of the too-much-too-soon trend, is encouraged by sophisticated mothers. If daughter is not dating by the time she is twelve Mother is asking the psychiatrist "Where did I fail?" The "smart" mother worries if her daughter gets home from a date too early. She fears that the child may be socially maladjusted or perhaps even retarded in boyology. Many mothers have become "call girls," sitting at the phone soliciting dates for their "shy" daughters. Shyness, which used to be considered becoming in a young girl, is now equated with backwardness. She must be popular at any price.

One psychiatrist recently reported that many mothers are buying "falsies" for their underendowed teen-age daughters to bolster their depressed egos. The mothers, wittingly or unwittingly, are forcing their daughters into positions where they may have to prove to some young road scholar how grown-up they are. What next? Little maternity gowns like Mother's?

The schools have been pressured into preparing the girls for the mating game. Schools now must teach social dancing or run the risk of losing their academic accreditation.

You cannot encourage social dancing at the age of nine (or earlier) without encouraging sex sophistication at the same time. For social dancing you need a partner. A girl is not going to dance with a girl. She would flunk the course. So able-bodied though reluctant young boys are drafted into the Dance Corps.

There are other social graces besides dancing that can be taught to young people: feeding the sick, helping the retarded, reading to the blind.

If some mother feels that all this glandular stimulation is just a bit premature, that not all adult sports must have a Little League, she will probably be victimized by the "smart" mothers. It usually works like this: the girl comes to Mama and says "Look, Ma. Shirley's mother lets her. Why do you have to be so old-fashioned? You're from the olden times. Didn't they have parties when you were alive, Mom?" Shirley's mother is the type who brags, "My little girl is no sleepyhead." She's probably no little girl, either. Every community has a few of these Shirley's mothers—wildcat organizers of the Teensters' Union who demand seniority without maturity.

Shirley's mother makes another mistake. She provides

the kind of *dolce vita* atmosphere that offers more temptations than a motel. "I don't want my kids out there somewhere away from home where they can drink, and smoke
and God knows what. I like to know where they are at
all times." So she provides a nice, clean place at home
where they can drink and smoke and God knows what.
"So long as I know *where* she is," says Shirley's mother. It
is wise to remember what the safety councils say: "Most
accidents happen at home." Dr. Kinsey, too, indicated that
most teen-age initiation parties take place at home. As
that famous housekeeper said, "A house is not a home"—
but a home can be converted into a house by parents who
have forgotten that the teens are the age of great passions.
It is all very well to have faith in your daughter, but someone should keep an eye out for biology, which thrives on
dim lights, soft couches, romantic music, strong drinks and
seclusion. Shirley's mother should also be reminded that
if Shirley gets into "trouble" she will blame her mother—
not the dim lights, or the soft couch, or the romantic
music, or the strong drinks, or the boy. As for the boy, he
will hate Shirley. He may even marry her but he will still
hate her. Actually the "first" boy rarely marries the "first"
girl.

Concerning the prom, which is the greatest social event
in the life of a high school student and the longest night
in the life of a parent (between the hours of 9 and 1 P.M.
parents have been known to age thirty years), I would
suggest this rule of thumb: Permit neither excess of time,
liquid stimulation, or opportunity to bring about a sudden collapse of the future of the child you have lovingly
raised to maturity. Trial by orgy is not a fitting gradua-

tion exercise. As one wise parent put it: "Our senior prom is supervised by an adult young enough to know what a bunch of healthy, exuberant young people might like to do, and so see to it that they don't do it."

❀❀❀❀

To the teen-agers' complaint that we cannot possibly understand them because we grew up in the equivalent of King Arthur's court, we must tell them candidly that when it comes to sex we do understand. The demands of our bodies were as great when we were young as theirs are now. We faced the same great physical stresses and had to fight off the same teen-age hunger in our limbs. Above all we must admit that it is not easy. We extend our sympathy and our best wishes.

Every dogma has its day. Today the early-to-bed dogma seems to be recruiting hosts of devout adherents. The sexperts recommend teen-age relations to the full on the grounds that it is natural and honest, therefore moral. To deny this natural urge, they say, is an act of hypocrisy that will leave the adolescent a mass of inhibitions which will in time be transmitted to his own children. All that is required of the practitioners of this philosophy is sincerity and one partner at a time. One at a time is love. Two is promiscuous. With three it's sexual independence, and beyond that, research. All this sexual activity is known as playing it cool, a passionate commitment to no commitment.

Society has derived one great benefit from the sexual-

EVERYTHING BUT MONEY

freedom-for-teen-agers movement. It has virtually wiped out prostitution. The amateurs have killed the business.

What do you tell a sophisticated generation of teen-agers about babies? How do you foster in them a high regard for their creative powers, sexual or otherwise? Scare them into abstinence with statistics about illegitimacy? While teen-agers do not scare easily, the numbers are becoming more frightening each year. There are some 250,000 illegitimate babies born each year in the United States. The rate has tripled in the last twenty-five years. One out of twenty babies is born out of wedlock, not in an age of ignorance but in an age of enlightenment in which teen-agers *know* where babies come from. "Nice" families are represented as well as "bad" ones.

Whether these babies are born of burning love or burning sex or both or neither, they are not welcomed into the world. This catastrophe is intensified by the fact that the offering of one's self, the supreme act of cherished privacy shared in love, has in most such instances been degraded to the animal level. Birth, the most exalted moment of life, here becomes only an undesirable consequence. The youthful dream of self re-created through love becomes a lifelong nightmare.

The plight of the unmarried teen-age father is just as serious as that of the mother. While the world tends to regard only the girl as "in trouble," this traumatic experience will affect the boy's future development, his education, his marriage, and possibly destroy the message he was born to deliver. Boys, along with girls, should be made aware of the enormous price to be paid for getting into trouble. While abortion or forced marriage may solve the

254

immediate problem, it leaves emotional scars for life. All the lives involved have been aborted. For teen-agers the most completely dependable oral contraceptive is "No."

We are an enlightened people and everybody agrees that children should be told the facts of life, but what are *the* facts? It is easy to draw a diagram and indicate where the little sperm goes to keep its rendezvous with the little egg, but are these all the facts?

If you are going to teach a child about the nature of human life it is essential that from the minute he begins to "wonder" he be introduced bit by bit to the wonder of life and of love. Unless you have transmitted to the child an attitude of reverence, you have merely been discussing plumbing.

Teen-agers will become involved in sexual experiences. The best we can do for them is to give them a philosophy that will help them handle the lust for life with dignity. A teen-ager involved in an undress rehearsal ought to know that he is playing with fire—the fire of life. Stirring within him is the magnificent life force, hard to define but easy to defile. On its way from eternity to eternity it passes through our bodies. We can either drink from the sacred stream of life or pollute it.

The youngster will exercise self-restraint if he has been taught to approach sex with awe. He will move normally toward genuine love and genuine marriage when he realizes that the mysterious power which moves him to love is the same power that moves the universe. This power has many names: God, Nature, Love, Omnipotence, Omniscience, Truth, Mind, Spirit, Supreme Being, Essence, Life, First Cause. There are hundreds of names which man the theologian as well as man the scientist, in search of the secret of his own life, has given to this force. It is the intelligent recognition of it and homage paid to it that distinguishes man from beast.

A girl who realizes that her body is a private treasure and not a public playground is prepared to make her debut.

❀❀❀❀

Girls are under great pressure to marry young. Another trend. We are reverting to the primitive requirement for marriage—physical maturity. The Wasserman test is now often given by the pediatrician, along with other booster shots. A girl of twenty who is "not married or anything" is generally considered to be over the hill. Graduation from college without a husband (or at least, a signed-up undergraduate) is dangerous ("I've been in college for four years, and whom has it got me?"). One mother said to me, "I figured, let her get married. She wasn't doing well in school and she was too young to go to work." While the mothers will not admit it openly they are frightened by the statistics on premarital pregnancies and would prefer to have their little girl married "rather than."

Girls are urged to be early settlers: "Make up your mind"; "Don't be too choosy"; "Ask him to stay over"; "Don't bury your nose in your books"; "How long is he going to drag you around?"; "You're not getting younger, you know."

"What do you want me to do, take the first guy who comes along?"

"Take the second, but take!"

Almost any male animal who strays into the house is judged to be a "lovely boy." "They have a lot in common." (Both have braces on their teeth.)

A new set of pre-engagement customs has emerged: pinnings, friendshipings, charmings, pledgings, keyings, remembrancings, keepsakings. No girl, however, feels secure until there is a stoning.

Marriage is not for children. The selection of a mate depends more on intellectual and emotional maturity than upon being physically ready. There is a good chance that the man a girl picks at the age of eighteen would not be the one she would pick at twenty-one. The divorce rate among teen-agers is higher than among most other age groups. The age between eighteen and twenty-one should be left free for serious consideration of the kind of adult life one would like to lead and the kind of mate with whom one would like to lead it. Besides, there ought to be a few years of grace before marriage in which both parties should have the right to a change of mind.

If we mean what we say about providing the best possible environment for individuals to develop to their highest potential, we should discourage too abrupt a switch from fraternity pins to diaper pins. The normal conditions of marriage: pregnancy, children, laundry, dishes, measles, arguments, rent, repairs, bills, in-laws and jobs—are hardly normal conditions for the further growth of a teen-ager.

I do not believe in undergraduates marrying in college. It creates too many problems for the youngsters and their parents. The college years should be exempt from serious emotional and financial encumbrances. "Playing house" and serious study don't go well together. Too many young men have had to alter the course of their careers to meet the needs of house and home. Even when parents can afford to subsidize such marriages the psychological effect has not been good. The "kept" husband very often develops feelings of sexual and financial inadequacy. The young woman may cut her education short to further her husband's career. He then develops guilt feelings about her sacrifices.

True love can wait—for a better time, for a job, and for the sheer satisfaction of marrying without sacrifices on the part of one's mate or parents. There is a great joy in making it on your own. It is an excellent basis for marriage.

❀❀❀❀

The American passion for college education can be divided into two historic periods: B.S. and A.S.—Before Sputnik and After Sputnik. We had to catch up with Russia and Russia had to catch up with us. True education has nothing to do with such power struggles. It should be concerned only with the individual's catching up with his own potential. In this sense all people are capable of "higher" education, but all do not necessarily have to get it at college.

The college panic starts in nursery school. Parents know just how many graduates of Peter Pumpkin-on-the-Hudson made it to Harvard. Children are made college-conscious from their first day at school. By the time they reach high school competition becomes savage. Love of learning, which should be the basic motivation, has been replaced by cramming for marks. Averages are read like stock-market reports: up .7%, down .37%. Parents pressure teachers for higher marks, earned or unearned—"But he is going to college." High school students become college-admissions hipsters who know all about percentiles, upper half, lower half, quotas, scores, early acceptance, late acceptance, waiting lists. . . .

Emergency educational institutions have sprung up all over the country: the B.A. (Before Application) coaching academies whose urgent curriculum consists of How to Lick the College Boards. The crash program consists mostly of hysterical training in blank filling, multiple choices, checking off, speed reading, vocabulary enrichment, en-circling, key words, tricks, devices, memory aids—all of which are frowned upon by the colleges. One college-admissions officer tells of receiving an application blank from a boy who was so well coached in underlining that in answer to the question "Do you believe in the over-throw of the United States government by force or vio-lence?" he underlined the word "violence." Terror-stricken parents refuse to believe the truth—that there *is* a place for any reasonably equipped student who is anx-ious to go to college. But this is not what so many parents are looking for. It must be the *right* college. It is *their* status which is at sake, not *his*. I know high school prin-cipals who promote this kind of status seeking in their students. It gives the school "class." I have seen daily scoreboards mounted in school corridors announcing Ivy League acceptance victories: Smith 2, Yale 1—followed by a cheering-squad demonstration in the auditorium.

Tourism is also profiting from the passion for college education. Parents and child take trips to look over the college which has not yet decided whether it wants him. They inspect the campus, check on the condition of the ivy, the cleanliness of the dormitories, the equipment of the laboratories, the geographic availability of the opposite sex and the unavailability of transportation to make sure that the children see as little of their parents as possible in the next four years. Going to college as far away from home as possible is the ultimate in separatism. The better the home the farther the child must get from it. After graduation, status requires an apartment of one's own to avoid living among parents who have by now become his intellectual inferiors.

There is much fact and fancy about what will get a youngster into college. Basically it comes down to this: the kid needs good marks and the father needs good money. All the rest are variations on this theme.

One of the popular college-entrance clichés is "well-roundedness." Like the meatball, which is also well-rounded, the applicant must contain a little bit of everything. One young man got so involved in debating, fencing, swimming, stamps and cheering that he forgot how to read.

The pages in the college catalogue dealing with entrance requirements are enough to scare a kid to death. Half the people listed in Who's Who couldn't get into college today. The applicant now has to possess the scientific genius of an Albert Einstein and the all-around development of a Zsa Zsa Gabor. "Send $50 with application." If not accepted, the application will be refunded; the money will not.

Generally disregarded by most parents is the simple consideration of the intellectual and emotional needs of the child, and the importance of providing him with an educational environment which will encourage him to deliver *his* personal message to the world—not theirs.

We should stress "calling" more than "career." Of all the offenses committed in the name of higher education the most insidious is the practice by guidance and Government bureaus of listing the amounts of money that can be earned in the various professions. They sound like bribes, as do the radio and TV public-service announcements that proclaim: "An educated man earns more than an uneducated man." They are misleading and materialistic. This kind of logic puts teachers in the category of the uneducated. Some of the most educated men in the world earn little, and some of the least educated have become millionaires. Self-advancement is not quite the same as advancement of one's self. Salaries are an economic rather than a cultural problem. Education should not be promoted by the family or the country as a stepping-stone to financial success but as the means to a richer life in its richest sense.

❀❀❀❀❀

For the college graduate, male, the world today offers great opportunities. For the college graduate, female, there are almost equal opportunities, and more than equal agonies. The problem becomes more acute each year as more and more women attempt to combine careers with matrimony only to find out that the problems of home and children fall to her. What happens to the right to self-fulfillment, which is as much hers as her husband's? She was promised the world. She is a free, thinking, educated, emancipated woman, with a message to deliver. She is different from her mother, whose world was limited to the home. She is at home in the arts, music, literature, science and philosophy. She is, in fact, at home everywhere but at home. At the age of twenty-one, holding a diploma full of career promises in one hand and a marriage license full of romantic promises in the other, she is carried over the threshold—into the kitchen. This is the true "commencement."

For a year or two everything works out fine for the young couple. They are both working. He picks up the newspaper; she picks up the TV dinner. There are quick fun meals, rich desserts, much talk about their respective jobs, and much honeymooning. This is the college dream come true.

Then comes the baby, and with it the explosion of the equal-rights principle. Motherhood is the one career for which she has had virtually no training. While the possibility of such an eventuality was vaguely mentioned in college, it was just one of those remote bridges to be crossed if and when she got to it.

She is now trapped at home. He is out in the free world. She becomes jealous of his freedom. He comes home at 6 P.M. to greet this prematurely old young lady, her dark hair highlighted with farina sprinkles, a strong-smelling kid on her arm, and anything but a Mona Lisa smile on her lips. She thinks, four years in college for this? He takes one look at her and he thinks, Oh, boy. What I married! and politely kisses her between the smudges. If she can afford full-time help she becomes jealous of the child's natural affection for the mother-substitute. The child, naturally, has learned to love the hand that feeds it. The mother is afraid of losing the love of her child. She wants to be a mother. She also wants to have a career. Grandma had a saying about this dichotomy: "You can't sit at two weddings with one fanny."

Her job is more difficult than her husband's. He has the greatest "out" in the world. He is making a living for the family. He can leave the scene of the crime every morning with the approval of the whole world. She cannot. She would trade places with him gladly, but she makes a noble attempt at homemaking, a career which, she hopes, will eventually provide the same satisfactions as the chemistry laboratory.

She gets down to the business of being an "enlightened" mother, of fulfilling the multiple roles expected of her: wife, mistress, and delightful companion in the evening; and, with the rising sun, chauffeur, shopper, interior decorator, crabgrass puller, den mother, PTA-er, bazaar chairlady. She appears to herself as a cubist painting of a mother and child: two heads, four eyes, three ears, four bosoms, one baby, mandolins, pots, pans, microscopes, diplomas and the death mask of a college girl.

Meanwhile, back at the lab, there's her husband, the all-American boy, whose unmarried secretary looks like his wife used to. She's pretty and young and calm. No kid has vomited into her typewriter, and she has the freedom, time and availability that his wife has sacrificed —in the service of his home.

The frightened wife picks up the challenge. She's got

to look and behave like a seductive secretary. She colors her hair, lowers her neckline, heightens her heels, shortens her dresses, lengthens her eyelashes to re-entice her husband, whose sense is coming out with his hair. He thinks he has remained handsome, irresistible, the eternal Don Juan. The wife knows he's behaving like an idiot, but she mercifully keeps the news from him.

The conflict in the mind and heart of the college-educated married woman is only one more aspect of the problem of individual fulfillment of one's greatest gifts. To deny selfhood to a woman because she is married and a mother leads to profound unhappiness, a nagging sense of "might have been," and too often a resentment against the husband and children who lured her away from her true mission in life. The torturous division of loyalties inflicted upon this woman by our ambiguous promises of equality of opportunity for both sexes leads many women to the psychiatrist.

The easy answer is to proclaim that woman's mission in life is to be a mother. Most women want to be mothers, but they were also trained for many other professions. Is it possible to be a good chemist and a good mother? Can a mother be in two places at the same time? What about the needs of the children? And what about the country's need for talent of all kinds? If women were intended by nature to be mothers, why does nature also endow them with intellectual gifts equal to those of the men? And what right have men to ask their mates to deny their talents and devote themselves to housekeeping?

Some people have suggested that a woman should get a full education, then marry, raise her children, and after about ten years, go back to her career. The children would then be taken care of by some member of the family, or a maid. The chances of resuming her career after ten years, however, are not very good.

Perhaps the husbands of such women should stay home and raise the children. The husband as breadwinner is only a convention based on the assumption that he is the stronger of the two. In this age of technology we don't need strong people; we need skilled people.

Perhaps there should be all-day schools that would take care of the children from 7 A.M. to 6 P.M.

Perhaps women should postpone going to college until after their children are old enough to be looked after by others.

Perhaps those college girls who feel very intensely about a life devoted to science or the arts should be encouraged not to get married at all.

At any rate, we have worked ourselves into a situation we did not anticipate when we proclaimed liberty and justice for all and built an educational system to promote it. Perhaps we did not truly believe that woman could become the equal of man. Well, she is, and, in many instances, superior. Man had better find a just way of giving her her due.

There are many fine mothers who want to stay at home but are forced by economic necessity to neglect their children and go out to work. Society should subsidize these women adequately and keep them at home. We cannot have Papa on the night shift and Mama on the day shift, leaving kids to shift for themselves.

There are also many mothers who use work as an excuse

to get away from the responsibilities of home. They rationalize themselves into a job that will provide the "luxuries" they claim the children need. Most children would rather have the mother at home than any "luxury." A key to the house is not a substitute for the welcome of a mother at the door. Unwarranted mother absenteeism is an unhealthy condition in the home. I am not talking about leaving the children with Grandma or some other competent and devoted person while the parents grab a few hours or days together. I do refer to chronic neglect in so-called "rich" homes where children of educated parents are being raised by semiliterate strangers. It does not make much sense for an intelligent mother, presumedly aware of the emotional, aesthetic, spiritual and physical needs of children to turn hers over to the care of a housekeeper. One of the most revealing comments was made by a youngster who, when his mother said, "Don't tell me what to do. I know how to bring up children," replied: "You do? Were you once a maid, Mom?"

☙☙☙☙☙

While we are on the subject of work we cannot avoid discussing another "trend"—inferior workmanship.

The labor movement has been responsible for one of America's greatest achievements, the raising of the standard of living of the workingman to the highest level in the world. I remember only too well the sweatshop horrors to which my father's generation was subjected: the insecurities, exploitations and indignities imposed on unprotected human beings. The work, however, needs as much protection as the worker. It is becoming increasingly difficult to find a workingman who takes pride in his job, who takes the time required to do it well, and stands behind it. While the labor union must provide every economic and social protection for the worker, it must also protect the work itself. To get a good job has become more important than to do a good job. The dignity of labor is part and parcel of the quality of labor. The Old Testament (Proverbs) says: "He who is slack in his work is a brother to him who destroys."

We have become accustomed to substandard painting, plumbing, carpentry, automobile repairs, take-it-or-leave-it workmanship, and to paying out money to people who did not truly earn or deserve it.

If time has become a labor commodity with a price value on it, why should it be squandered? The sight of a workingman stretching a fifteen-minute job to three hours is degrading to labor. There is something profoundly dishonest about a man pretending to be at work, making a mockery of creative ability. With the passing of time men will earn more and more money and derive less and less joy from their work as it will come to represent less of themselves.

The contribution of the creative man to society is being undermined by the deliberate creation of second-rate merchandise. The gap between the creator-artisan and his consumer-patron has been widened to the point where not only don't we know each other, we no longer respect each other.

Big business as well as little business has become "irresponsible" for its product in the basic semantic sense— not answerable. The consumer's fight for justice becomes a whodunit. The man with the broken toaster, a victim of organized irresponsibility, is left to figure out his rights in a welter of guarantees, warranties, certifications, assurances, endorsements, and seals of testing laboratories which do or do not include parts, do or do not include labor charges, do or do not include mailing costs (I have been asked to mail a sixty-pound "portable" hair dryer to another state for repairs).

The lexicon of questionable workmanship is becoming richer and more deceptive as the work gets poorer. In case of a functional or constructional failure these dubious documents are presented to a man who never made the product, who in turn must contact a distributor, who must contact a jobber, who must contact some elusive figure who is "not with us any more." If you can track down the manufacturer at all, so much time has elapsed that he can tell you in all truth that "we don't make that model no more."

Not only do our appliances wear out prematurely; they also wear us out before our time. My wife and I have seen some weird irregularities develop in our "conveniences." Our freezer threw us a surprise housewarming. It overheated and cooked sixty pounds of meat and vegetables. Our washing machine skipped a cycle, dried the laundry first, rinsed it, then went mad and foamed at the mouth.

We need the leisure time automation gives us—time to search the Yellow Pages for the names of men to keep our conveniences in good health. (Estimates for repairs on the same product range from two dollars to four hundred.) Our devices have to be serviced by specialists who somehow manage to show up just in time for the death of the guarantee.

"Your guarantee just expired."

"Why didn't you notify us, the immediate family, that it was dying?"

The repairman is always a bit edgy but polite. He addresses the client as "lady," even if it is a man.

"Lady, who sold you this load?"

(He did, but you're afraid to tell him for fear that he might not want to repair it at all.)

"Lady, this model was never no good."

"Lady, you touched it." (The consumer must never touch the product.)

"I promise never to touch it again if you promise to repair it."

"It can't be done—here, lady."

"Why not?"

"I don't have the parts—here, lady."

"How much are the parts?"

"I can't tell—here, lady."

"Forget it."

"O.K. That's $7.50—here, lady."

"For what?"

"That's the minimum consultation service charge for an hour, lady."

⠿⠿⠿

I have found it easier to keep my body in repair than my house. It is much more difficult to get a plumber than a doctor. I discovered, in fact, that they have the same answering service. Here is a transcript of my phone conversation with Mr. Flushman the plumber's answering service.

OPERATOR: Mr. Flushman's office. Mr. Flushman is not in at the moment. He is out on an emergency case. We expect to hear from him or his associate.

ME: May I request an audience with him as soon as possible?

OPERATOR: May I ask your problem?

ME: You mean you'd like my symptoms? I've got water on my knees, both of them, and it's moving up my back. Talk fast!

OPERATOR (writing while mumbling): Has lost control of water.—Where can you be reached?

ME: Try Underwater 6–2000; ask for Bubbles Levenson.

OPERATOR: May I suggest that you shut off all the water lines until you hear from us?

Three days later I had to defrost the front door to let in the mailman. On the fourth day our boiler went dead. This time I got the Master Plumber himself on the phone:

ME: We're freezing. No heat.

HE: Can't touch it.

ME: Why not?

HE: Not my jurisdiction.

ME: Whose jurisdiction is it?

HE: Long Island Lighting.

I called Long Island Lighting. "Sorry, that's not our jurisdiction. Call your plumber." I called him, and because of what I called him he refused to come. He sent his intern.

Unlike the master plumber, the intern doesn't need an answering service; he uses the client's phone. "Any messages for me, Mr. Levenson?"

"Yes. Call your mother-in-law, then your sister, then Mr. Flushman."

He talked on the phone for two hours, then went to lunch. I didn't go to lunch. I couldn't leave the house. I had to take messages.

After he came back he cross-examined me. "Any messages? What? Who is he? What time did he call? You've got the wrong exchange. I may lose the job now. Can't you write better than that? You, a schoolteacher?"

He fixed the radiator but left his hammer—inside. It bangs every morning at 6 A.M.

"You got steam, ain't you? So don't complain," he says.

I got hold of an electrician who agreed to electrocute the plumber.

Meanwhile I have suggested a bill to my Congressman—Bill /2657/a, "A Proposal for Socialized Plumbing."

🕸🕸🕸🕸🕸

My experience with dry cleaners has been no less nerve-racking. My wife sent me to this particular shop with her dress because the sign in the window said ANY GARMENT CLEANED—79¢. 24-HR. SERVICE. The nice girl made out a pink slip to read 1 Blue Dress—$1.25. I didn't notice the price until I got home.

My wife asked, "Why $1.25?"

"I don't know."

"Go back and tell them it's a mistake."

I went back.

"Well, you see, sir, this dress has buttons."

"So?"

"So that's extra. I'm not charging you for the belt. If the boss finds out, I'll get plenty."

I was so pleased to get my wife's belt cleaned for free that I let it go.

"When shall I come for the dress?"

"It will take about four days."

"Four days? What happened to the 24-Hr. Service?"

"Oh, you want the Special Service. It costs only twenty-five cents more. Would you like to insure the garment?"

"You expect a fire?"

"No. We insure it against loss."

"You mean you expect to lose it?"

"Of course not. Just in case, that's all. It's optional."

Being a worrier I took out insurance.

She called out the presser as a witness.

"Place your right hand on the pink slip and repeat slowly after me: 'We are not responsible for nylons, rayons, buckles, buttons. I promise not to argue with the counter-girl.' You may go now."

Scene 2. One Week Later

My wife called for the dress. "What's this stain here in front?"

"It must have been there when you brought it in."

"That's why I brought it in, but it's still there."

"It must be a fruit stain."

"That's good to know, but I want it out. Send it back."

"We can't remove the stain, but we can move it to some place where it doesn't show. Do you want the special or regular service?"

"Never mind. I'll wash it myself."

"In that case you owe us only seventy-nine cents."

⊗⊗⊗⊗⊗

"The whole world is watching America, and America is watching TV."—Folk Saying, U.S.A.

Technology has produced the greatest instrument for mass education—television. What it will do to and for the individual mind in the coming decades may determine the future of the human race.

It has already altered the appearance of the American home inside and out. Outside, all dwellings, even tenements, now look like shrines capped by aluminum crosses —symbol of the new cult of darkness. Inside, all chairs and all people face in the direction of the electronic eternal light.

The clock on the wall no longer serves as a measure of time but as a guide to the beginning and end of TV programs. "It's ten minutes to Casey, Mom." Clocks may sometimes be late, but "What's My Line" never is. The sun rises with "Today" and sets with "Tonight," followed by sixty seconds of taped prayer for peace on earth and TV for all men.

Americans are supposed to be a fairly healthy, attractive people. By the standards of TV commercials, however, we are indeed "ugly Americans." We are reminded day in and day out that we have wobbly dental plates, flaky scalp, greasy valves, clogged pores, stuffed sinuses, undernourished skin, acid-ridden intestines and bad breath. Any viewer who has all of these conditions can qualify for the Sponsor's Pin-up Girl of the Month contest.

Of all commercials, I resent most those which are planned to capitalize on man's sexual drives. Toothpaste gets you a woman, cars get you a woman, razor blades get you a woman. To promise sexual pleasure to a man if he buys a particular product is procuring.

How is the great new medium affecting the lives of our children? It is the use we adults make of it that will determine the good or evil effect it will have on them. It can do wonders for the child. How many ballets did I ever see as a child? How many dramatic performances, operas, musical comedies, historical documentaries, inaugurations? Very few indeed. Today's child can see them. Life in the TV box is the image of life in the world outside. Fine art and low art exist there in about the same proportions as they do in the world outside the box. We, the parents, must do the selecting—if we have the courage.

Selective viewing falls into the same category as selecting the clothes we want our children to wear, the books we want them to read, the movies we want them to see, the friends we want them to have, the museum we would like them to visit, the hours we would like them to keep. Parents who feel that TV can do more than it does now for the aesthetic, emotional and intellectual growth of their children should use the democratic pressures available in a free society. They should tell the sponsor what they want and, even better, watch the good shows themselves to make sure their ratings go up. The schools should list the shows they think will do the children the most good under "Preferred Viewing for Our Children" and send such a list home to the parents.

In most homes the child does his own selecting. All the

mother has to do is feed him intravenously every four hours so he doesn't collapse in front of the set. Too many parents are using TV as an electronic baby-sitter. To leave a child in his TVD's in front of a TV set without supervision is as dangerous as leaving him in front of an open medicine cabinet. He may reach for vitamins, but he may also swallow poison. The amount of viewing by children should be limited in the interest of leaving plenty of time for reading, homework, music lessons, sports and just plain thinking. Doing homework in front of the TV set should never be permitted.

The image of the father in most situation comedies does not help to strengthen the position of the live father at home. The TV daddy is a genuine shnook, a bungler who has to be saved from destroying himself in the last three minutes of each episode. The "problems" in such family comedies are as earth-shattering as "Does Wendy get to wear the high heels at the prom?" or "How to break the news to Daddy that his daughter is not going to play the piano at the Rotary Club luncheon." There is one thing that can be said for those energetic families on TV —they don't sit around watching TV.

What about the exposure to violence? Will it make gangsters of our children? It will undoubtedly influence the attitude of the emotionally sick child who is seeking an outlet for his hostilities. The ordinary kid will not imitate the violence he sees on TV.

Something worse is happening, not only to children, but to their parents—a growing indifference to bloodshed. We are being desensitized by overexposure to brutality. Even those cute little characters in the cartoons are constantly banging each other on the head, pushing each other off cliffs, going up in explosions, getting hit by trains—but they always recover immediately. Maybe this explains why a group of people can stand by and watch a woman being beaten on the street and not get involved. It's just another scene.

What happens to the individual and his special message under the impact of commercial TV? Since it is a "mass" industry, it caters to the "average" man, who is not regarded as an individual at all but as a statistic. Its goal is to reach the greatest number of people for the greatest amount of time. The argument is used that for the "unusual" man there is educational television. Our answer is that every man is potentially unusual. It was Emerson who said, "A weed is a plant whose virtues have not been discovered." Who knows how much of value there is in the despised weed unless we make a true effort to extract its virtues?

Schoolteachers use a bell curve to represent the range of intelligence in an average classroom. There is a round-topped mountain in the middle representing the majority, and a flattening out at both ends of the slopes representing about equal amounts of high-grade and low-grade mental ability. The television audience can be charted in much the same manner—the great mass in the middle, and the usual lows and highs at the beginning and end of the curve. This curve describes with considerable reliability what the intellectual status of the viewing group is *at the time of the sampling*—but it is in a constant state of flux. Ordinary minds can become unusual and move toward the smart end of the curve. They can also move in the other direction and become dull, duller, or dullest. The direction they take depends very much upon the effort made to move them. In TV the effort must be made by the performing artist, the writer, the producer, and the television executive. They are all teachers. They must be ever mindful of the potential of the man in the middle of the curve. It is essential to create programs for him (in prime time) not as he *is,* but as he might *become.* It is cynical and irresponsible to treat him as unimprovable. Democracy is based on the premise that he *is* improvable.

Most of the men who make policy in television have good taste. Their homes are filled with good art and good music, yet they live by a double standard of culture. As soon as they get to the office they seem to leave their fine taste behind. They start creating for the masses what is "good enough for *them.*"

I should like to bring attention to two projects sponsored by the Board of Education of the City of New York which have proved beyond any doubt that the cultural level of the ordinary and less than ordinary man can be raised. First, the Higher Horizons program which showed the "them" type of students a world they had never seen before—a world of concerts, museums, rehearsals, operas, industrial shows, art shows, libraries. . . . The minds of these children were prodded into functioning on their highest rather than their lowest level. Many were stimulated enough to go on to higher education. All discovered the joy of contact with the thinking world.

The Friends of Music of the Junior High Schools, an educational project in which I am personally involved, gave children from poor as well as comfortable homes the opportunity to create music in choral groups, bands and orchestras. I saw several thousand children go from musical deprivation (yes, even among the rich) to Mozart's "In Excelsis" within one year. These children will never be the same. They will demand more of themselves and of the world because we believed in their potential for greatness. It can be done.

The television industry should look at itself at least once a day and instead of asking "What harm can it do?" ask "What good can it do?"

IV
"My dear children"
❁❁❁❁

I T IS IRONICAL that at the peak of our automated-mecha-nized-instant-quick-frozen civilization the items that move off the supermarket shelves fastest are the ones labeled "Like Mama Used to Make." More and more cans, jars and packages now carry a picture of a short, plump, gray-haired, old-fashioned grandma offering herring, noodles, bread, cake, meatballs like only she can make. It looks as though Grandma may be "in" again. Are we merely trying to recapture the taste sensations or with them the emotions of a simpler era? Is it the hot soup we are after, or the warmer life? Perhaps we are also trying to revive some of Mama's values along with her cooking.

Those values were not based upon a recipe but upon faith in her instincts and experience. Her values, like her cooking, contained a pinch of this, a twist of that, a lick, a smell, a dab, a drop, a smack, a snip or a scoop. Somehow this all added up to an identifiable philosophy far more exact than the fragments that went into it.

In Mama's home we were fed on these principles:

An unfavorable environment can be overcome by challenging it every inch of the way, through individual and group effort. To make a separate peace with poverty, filth, immorality or ignorance is treason to the rest of the human race.

Spiritual poverty can be as devastating as material poverty. Thing-worship is not far removed from idol-worship. More or larger is not necessarily better.

Old can be as good as new. The latest is not always the best. While the past is not sacred merely because it is the past, neither is the present to be honored because it is here and now. Today can be worse than yesterday. Progress can be made by looking back as well as ahead.

All education must be based upon the morality of the brotherhood of man, and the brotherhood of man begins in this house on this block.

You will finally have to do it yourself: free yourself, educate yourself, support yourself.

Parents are responsible for the behavior of their children.

Since I believe that these principles are still valid, I should like to pass them along to my children with a few additions of my own:

My dear children:

Do not "play it cool." Get involved. Now is the time for all good men to come to. Men of good will are inclined to take freedom for granted. They believe that freedom, like the sun, will rise every morning. History has proved that it can be blacked out for decades. I have found that the people with the greatest amount of formal education are generally the least involved in the small but necessary details of preserving freedom. We are suffering from intellectual truancy at the grass-roots level. Men who have been trained to think do not generally offer their ability to do so to their immediate community. Free men should pay for their freedom in time and labor and money. Tom Paine said: "Those who expect to reap the blessings of freedom must undergo the fatigue of supporting it." Patriotism has as much to do with living for freedom as with dying for it.

Look with suspicion upon such slogans as "You can't argue with success." You can, and should. There are honorable ways of becoming a success, and ways that are legitimate but not quite honorable. The profit motive must be governed by moral restrictions. "Let the buyer beware" is a poor business philosophy for a social order allegedly based upon man's respect for his fellow man. Let the seller beware, too. A free-enterprise system not founded upon personal morality will ultimately lose its freedom.

Apply the time-tested principles of good family living to the family of man. As the world gets smaller, the similarity between the individual family and the world family becomes clearer. Individual nations, like individual members of a family, possess the same characteristics: some are more docile, some more belligerent, some are optimistic and outgoing, others are sullen and introverted, some require much attention, others very little; some feel, rightly or wrongly, that others in the family are being favored. Each has individual needs which a loving family should try to satisfy. As in the individual family, the least lovable are the ones who are in the greatest need of love.

In dealing with the world, ask yourself: "What would a good father, a good mother, a good brother or sister, a good family do in such a case?" Perhaps Grandma's approach to settling an argument among her children might work: It is not a question of who is right, but what is right, not who pushed whom first, but why must we push each other at all. Like Grandma, consider the possibility that both may be right or both wrong, and that a third premise may be needed, the premise of sacrifice in order to keep peace in the family.

Do not look upon the conquest of space as the beginning of the Messianic era. Like Grandma who cleaned the old apartment before she moved, before you leave this earth and move into outer space, take a hand in cleaning up some of the dirty spaces down here—the spaces between nations, religions, races. While all eyes are turned to the heavens in admiration of manmade celestial bodies, be sure to remember the manmade miseries; the two fifths of the human race that goes to bed hungry every night, the 50 per cent that cannot read or write, the bombings of homes and places of worship. Either our ethics keep up with our physics or we shall all be cremated equal.

The greatest hope for the human race is in the science of human relations, in the perfection of dependable formulas for human understanding, in the creation of giant laboratories in which the atom of hatred will be split and put to peaceful uses, in which antibodies will be discovered for personal and group violence, and observatories built in which the universe of the individual mind will be explored and charted. Our survival depends upon understanding the behavior of victims of prejudice, unemployment, poverty and ignorance. It depends also upon understanding and controlling the motivations, psychological, emotional or political, of those who seek to perpetuate human misery.

I would, above all else, urge you to remember your grandparents who envisioned America as the Great Society fifty years ago. Their dreams were the same as those of the founding fathers. Both valued freedom because they had known tyranny.

To my parents freedom meant above all, "Live and let live." They were willing to settle for tolerance as a way of life. For the world in which you are going to live, tolerance will not be good enough. We are now in the "Live and help live" era of democracy. Like your immigrant grandparents who sent for those left behind, you will have to help others to cross over into freedom.

🏵🏵🏵🏵🏵 About the Author

SAM LEVENSON *was raised and educated in New York. He holds a B.A. from Brooklyn College and an M.A. from Columbia University. He taught Spanish in the New York City high schools for fifteen years. During this period he also served for five years as a guidance counselor. He became a nationally known personality through his appearances on television and radio and had his own program, the Sam Levenson Show, on the Columbia Broadcasting System.*

Sam Levenson lectures frequently before civic, religious, fraternal, educational and community organizations throughout the country. He is married to his childhood sweetheart and is the father of a son and daughter.